SHOOTING PIGEONS

SHOOTING
PIGEONS

JOHN HUMPHREYS

Foreword by
ARCHIE COATS

David & Charles

BY THE SAME AUTHOR:

Living Off the Land
Hides, Calls and Decoys
The Sportsman Head to Toe
Modern Pigeon Shooting
Stanley Duncan, Wildfowler
The Shooting Handbook (Ed) 1983, 1984, 1985, 1986, 1990
The Do-It-Yourself Gameshoot
Learning to Shoot
The Woods Belong to Me (Ed)
Days and Nights on Hunter's Fen
The Complete Gundog
The Countrysportsman's Record Book & Journal
Poachers' Tales

Illustrations by John Paley, Dave Parfitt
and John Marchington

British Library Cataloguing in Publication Data

Humphreys, John
  Shooting pigeons.
  1. Pigeon shooting
  I. Title
  799.2'4865   SK325.P55

  ISBN 0-7153-9101-1

First published 1988
Second impression 1989
Third impression 1991
Fourth impression 1993

Typeset by ABM Typographics Limited, Hull
and printed in Great Britain
by Butler & Tanner Limited, Frome
for David & Charles
Brunel House   Newton Abbot   Devon

Contents

Dedication

I dedicate this book to the father of British pigeon shooting, the late Major Archie Coats. There can be no one branch of a field sport which has been so dominated by one man as has pigeon shooting by Archie. He shot more pigeons than anyone else in the country, for many years held the record bag of 550 birds in a session, wrote, lectured and made himself available to disciples at Game Fairs and thus educated two generations of pigeon shooters and put them on the right path.

Much of what is now accepted as standard practice and even the language of the sport, the 'sitty trees', the 'killing area' and also the deployment of decoys and construction of hides were first evolved by him.

Very few decoyed pigeons are shot without at least one of the Coats' tactics being used, whether the decoyer is aware of it or not.

I am one of thousands who owe many happy days in the pigeon field to the trail-blazing and the inspiration of Archie Coats.

J.H.

Archie Coats

Foreword

John has very kindly told me that he wishes to dedicate his new book to me. This is indeed a great honour, and I thank him for it — as I do for his articles in the *Shooting Times*, with which we can all identify, though my wife says this is a deplorable word.

I expect you will know what I mean when I say that perhaps the best thing about pigeon shooting is your own personal involvement. You and you alone can get it right or wrong.

John would be the first to agree that all those basic principles haven't changed, but you just have to think hard and get them absolutely right.

Don't forget, 'bangers' don't kill pigeons, you and I do!

The late Archie Coats
Dummer

Introduction

Bang! The three million and first pigeon to be shot over decoys this year collapses with a squirt of white feathers and, like a stricken bomber trailing smoke plunges down to thud onto the spring corn drill. Yes, the sport of pigeon shooting is very much alive and well in the UK, the only country to take woodpigeon shooting seriously, the cradle of the art of pigeon decoying and where the sport attracts flocks of new followers each year.

However, unlike pheasant shooting or wildfowling which evolved as far as they could and then settled down to an almost predictable routine, pigeon shooting is an ever-changing test. Methods which worked well even twenty years ago would be found wanting today. New crops, new farming practices, new decoys and hide materials, but most of all, new patterns of pigeon behaviour have made this so.

Those birds which, in the sixties, threw themselves so eagerly at your rather makeshift decoys and were so confident that they settled among them and could be shot on the ground (as many were) are creatures of the past. They were the ancestors

10

of modern woodpigeons which circle warily, which are put off by a careless hide or an unrealistic decoy and which feed at odd and unpredictable times of the day. My own best bag of 219 on a small field of badly drilled barley would be impossible now, for each of those birds was shot with a .22 rifle and short bullets as it settled. By the end of the afternoon the ten-acre (4ha) field looked as though a sudden fall of snow lay upon it, so thick were the feathers.

New pigeon behaviour is caused partly by the undiminished popularity of pigeon shooting and the constant exposure of pigeons to the decoyer's arts. The greedy, gullible and gregarious ones which filled our bags years ago were the first to be shot. Systematically eliminate those over a period of thirty years and it is the wary, the solitary and the suspicious ones which survive to pass on the genes of self-preservation to the next generation. There will be the odd throwbacks of course, but this unusual type of unnatural selection has evolved a pigeon of different behaviour patterns from its great, great, etc, grand-parents.

Now the birds feed in small, scattered flocks, by no means committed to the same field day after day until the food is exhausted. Sometimes they will descend in a great cloud, grab a few beakfuls and depart on a whim, not to return that day.

Another factor is the new farming scene, a picture which has changed radically and is due to change more before any of us is much older. Oilseed rape — pigeon man's friend or foe? The birds certainly love the stuff and I have seen flocks passing over perfectly good clover fields to attack the rape field next door. Clover too is becoming a rarer crop, peas are more popular, less corn is drilled in spring than in winter, and time was when the spring drilling was a sure-fire pigeon crop. The pigeon man must come to terms with these changes.

Enterprising inventors like Mr Richardson of the Market Deeping Woodpigeon Club and Allan Graham of Shooting Developments — to mention but two — are ever experiment-ing with new equipment which will help the pigeon decoyer keep a step ahead of a difficult quarry.

This little book looks at some methods, equipment and tac-tics which might be useful to the new recruit and it would give me great pleasure to think that even an older hand might dis-

Will Garfit and his bag of 271 pigeons shot at Hauxton, Cambridge-shire, in October 1986.

cover a wrinkle or two which will give him one or two better bags and turn a dud outing into a winner. Books on the subject are in surprisingly short supply. Max Baker's book *Shooting Woodpigeons* published in the 1930s is now hopelessly out of date; Archie Coats' *Pigeon Shooting* remains a classic but again, while his basics still hold true, much has changed in the pigeon-shooting world since it was published in 1954. The BASC (WAGBI) pamphlet suffers from a similar complaint and even the latest, my own *Modern Pigeon Shooting* (Tideline Books) has been rendered partly obsolete by the passage of a mere decade, and also some changes in my thinking.

Some of what follows is new stuff!

John Humphreys
Bottisham

1 · The Pigeon Shooter
and the Pigeon

The pigeon shooter tends to be a solitary type, happiest when on his own, carrying his own gear, making his own decisions and deciding for himself how best to go about things. Not for him the army of beaters, pickers up, keepers, drivers and helpers of the driven pheasant shoot, so he must be sturdy, if only to carry the heavy loads which have, by tradition, become part of the decoyer's lot. He is prepared to share an eighty-acre (32ha) rape field with a couple of pals, but he prefers to position himself as far away from them as possible — and ideally, in the best available place!

He may be sneered at by the tweedy set for being 'a market gunner', the ultimate insult, meaning one who shoots only to sell the bag and not purely for the joy of the sport. He comforts himself with the reflection that game shooters sell the bag and have done so for years in order to defray the hideous costs of their sport, so why shouldn't he do likewise? The acid test of a sporting decoyer is to see if he still goes out when the price of the birds is at rock bottom. A cartridge costs about 10p and an ace pigeon man might, on an exceptionally good day, kill one bird to two cartridges. At the time of writing, pigeon prices are suffering one of their increasingly frequent lows, and artificially depressed pigeon prices on the continent where most of our pigeons are sold. Next time, some other unconsidered factor will be held responsible and game dealers, with tears in their eyes, will indicate cold stores stuffed to overflowing with countless thousands of last year's pigeons.

Those shooters who persist in going out even at such times may not be held to be rapacious. Far from it, for they will certainly not recover the cost of their cartridges. Having said that, there is nothing wrong with selling the bag and now there are many game dealers who will take pigeons off your hands. In my young days there were a few secret addresses in the north of the country where they might be sent, in a sack on the train. In hot weather you risked losing the lot and at the best of times the price was in the lap of the gods, and I have been grateful to receive as little as two (very old) pence per bird.

The dreaded EEC regulations have struck even the humble pigeon man, for game dealers will now only take birds which weigh a minimum of 450 grammes and even if you have been canny and stored your birds in an old ice-cream freezer in the garage waiting until the price is right, the dealer may not take such birds at all. Try disposing of 250 half-thawed wood-pigeons one day, and you will quickly discover who are your true friends. Some crafty decoyers have been known to mix recently thawed birds with freshly shot ones, a dirty trick and one which in time will rebound only on them, as the dealer may refuse to take any of their birds, and the shooting grapevine is quick and sure. What is more, most game dealers I know were not born yesterday and are equal to all the tricks — no point in growing old unless you also grow cunning.

Local butchers will often take a few as will certain hotels, while discerning neighbours may be grateful for a handful. Unlike pheasants, no game dealer's licence is required for selling pigeons. Far better, in these days of lighter bags, is to keep them to eat yourself. By using the Ron Greenhill method, a pigeon may be rendered oven ready in forty seconds with no knife or scissors required, and in a later chapter in this book, the memsahib (author of *Game Cookery*, David & Charles) has provided some excellent new pigeon recipes to tempt the palate of the most discerning gourmet.

Woodpigeons are considered an agricultural pest, but let us not kid ourselves: a pigeon shooter rarely turns out simply in order to protect the farmer's crops. He may *say* he does and virtuously point out what a good job he is doing, but he has no incentive to protect a crop the success or failure of which will not affect him one way or the other. He goes because he likes it, because he is an enthusiast; he is not a poulterer but a connoisseur of an extremely tricky sort of shooting.

The pigeon man must not be afraid of solitude but be able to stand his own company, for he follows his sport in lonely places, on desolate arable acres and he must be prepared to sit in a hedge bottom for the best part of the day without growing bored, even though the 'action' might be slow. He will see the farm in every mood and in every season; he will develop an intimate knowledge of a wide tract of countryside round his home; he will be no mean naturalist, able to identify a distant

You will often see game from your hide. On no account touch it

Woodpigeon   Collared dove   Turtle dove

speck as stockdove, woodpigeon, kestrel, crow or gull — legal
proceedings might result from his making a mistake.

Once he has become accepted as part of the scenery on the
farms he shoots, the pigeon man becomes a privileged person.
In time he may find himself being asked to lend the keeper a
hand, to help with the rabbiting, to beat on shooting days and
eventually, if he is lucky, to carry his gun on an end-of-season
cock shoot. If he blots his copybook and leaves gates open, cuts
hardwood saplings for his hide, peppers the stock or, in a weak
moment, shoots a tempting pheasant, his permission will be
withdrawn a good deal more quickly than it was granted and
his reputation as an unreliable chap will go before him when he
tries to make overtures elsewhere. Country folk tend to have
long and retentive memories and a highly developed system of
communication.

I know a good many pigeon shooters and find them, like
coarse fishermen, patient, resourceful, practical, down-to-
earth and, by and large, good shots. Those in whom those
qualities are not well developed will be unlikely to make the
grade but will take up more congenial activities where success
is more predictable.

What then of the woodpigeon, the centrepiece of our concern and the grey hordes of which we dream at night coming in
boldly to our decoys? First we ought, perversely, to consider

Stockdove   *Rock dove*

his close relations for it is important to be able to tell the difference. The close cousin is the stockdove, protected by the 1981 Wildlife and Countryside Act by one of the crassest bureaucratic errors perpetrated in recent legislation. The bird is common, less gregarious than the woodpigeon, nests in hollow trees, survives in cold weather which kills woodpigeons in droves and is mistaken by the less experienced for its larger cousin. The stockdove is smaller, shorter-necked, darker in colour and has no white feather on its body. No-one who is really keen could confuse the two after a couple of days of close observation.

The stockdove will come to decoys, sometimes singly, sometimes as a pair. In the old days you could shoot one and put money on the fact that its mate would be round in the next five minutes to see where it had got to. You never shot a stockdove that was in anything but prime condition and they were, as they say round here, 'good eaters'. However, Laws is Laws, and the bird now enjoys full protection so that to shoot one might incur a heavy fine or even a spell in an hotel of Her Majesty's choice. Surely no-one would notice if I shot one or

(pages 18–19) *Woodpigeon drinking. This bird is the No 1 quarry of the pigeon decoyer;* (inset left) *Stockdove — protected since 1981;* (inset right) *Turtle dove — the voice of summer and strictly protected*

two, miles from anywhere, all alone in my camouflage netting. Don't you believe it! Bird-watchers with telescopes, passing farmers, keepers, hikers — the countryside is overlooked for most of the time and God's law dictates that the very moment you err, be it in the loneliest most remote of places, someone will see you. All country sportsmen must keep strictly to the Law.

Also protected is the delightful and migratory turtle dove whose delicate, serrated cooing makes pleasant the hot days of May, June and July, when 'the voice of the turtle is heard in the land'. The turtle dove will come to your decoys on certain crops, but its small size, brown speckles and quick, flicking flight make confusion with the woodpigeon impossible by any save the most inept. Anyone who shoots a turtle dove deserves jail for life, deporting to Botany Bay or instant execution, says I.

The one bird which *can* confound us is the closely related collared dove which can be confused with the turtle dove. The collared dove is one of the success stories of colonisation. Back in 1954 I shot one with an airgun, young savage that I was, and no-one had seen anything like it. 'Rare migrant' it said in my bird book, and I had it stuffed and preserved by that great taxidermist the late Tom Lee of Ely at a cost — horrendous in those days — of £20.00. How was I to know that during the next few years the bird was to become common, moving its range slowly and surely across Europe from east to west colonising, consolidating and becoming well established?

In the UK it was taken off the protected list when almost every suburban garden had its nesting pair, and its dry, breathy cooing early in the mornings drove the sleeping commuter to distraction and had him red-eyed and distraught, reaching for his son's air rifle. Later in the season they congregate in flocks and attack the mountains of grain which nowadays are piled loose in barns. What they do not eat they befoul, and they can be a real nuisance in this way. Their other favourite, when in the need of a little green salad, is to raid cottage and market gardens where they peck fruits and sprouting vegetables.

The collared dove tends not to work the open fields nor come into decoys, but good sport may be had with a 20-bore as they flit in and out of a barn or swoop down onto newly sprouting peas on your allotment. Please be careful when

Collared dove — not protected but not really a decoyer's bird

doing this, for a farmer prefers the depredations of any number of collared doves to having holes shot in his barn roof or his Sunday lie-in disturbed by your volley of bangs.

The rock dove is a dweller in sea caves, ancestor of the domestic pigeon, and was once shot from boats.

The real hero and subject of our story is the woodpigeon, cushat, cushy doo, doo or *columba palumbus*, a natural survivor in the animal kingdom. The woodpigeon population has variously been estimated at from ten to fifteen million birds, but goodness knows how such an estimate may be made in the light of great local migrations which are unpredictable, and also when influxes from the continent are likely in winter, a phenomenon still, however, open to doubt in the minds of many pigeon experts. Flocks have certainly been seen by longshoremen and lighthouse keepers flying in from the North Sea towards the Norfolk coast, but the sceptical maintain that the birds are merely migrating southwards from cold Scotland and have taken a short cut to East Anglia over the Wash. My own view is that it is likely that there does exist an element

Courting pigeons clatter from branch to branch

of migration from Scandinavia with flocks of small, dark-feathered pigeons following the redwings and fieldfares when autumn looks like becoming winter.

The pigeon is a large, powerful bird, generally grey in appearance with a pale pink breast, broad white stripe on the wing and a smart white collar. These white flashes are good distinguishing marks which, as we will see later, may be used to advantage when decoying. Wing tips and tail are darker, the latter having a black tip, and the underside feathers are almost white. Birds of the year are usually slimmer than their parents, of a duller colour and lack the white collar. Its call is a deep-throated cooing, a sound to be heard on *The Archers* throughout the summer, but to most country folk it is the accompaniment to woodland walks, picnics, and tea on the Vicarage lawn. The rhythmic cooing may be interspersed with a deep-throated purring call, instantly reminiscent of hot summer days. The pigeon calls only in the spring and summer months and to hear its first, half-hearted warming-up on a mild day in early March is as sure a harbinger of the changing season as the arrival of the cuckoo.

The calling is all part of the breeding cycle, and while pigeon nests with eggs have been found in every month of the year, peak nesting times are May and July. The nest is a flimsy cat's cradle of criss-crossed twigs low in a roadside thorn, elder bush or high up in a more substantial tree. The two, moon-white eggs are laid on this perilous platform and the squabs fed on a partly digested potage of food known as pigeon's milk. Farm boys in the old days would tether the squabs to the nest by means of a fine cord round the leg. The parents would continue to feed the young until they left the nest, but as they were unnaturally restrained from departing, they grew as fat as butter. Choosing his moment, the lad would bag the birds and his mother would make him a dish which for flavour and tenderness left roast pheasant as an also-ran.

A flimsy platform of twigs

Pigeon-egg custard was also popular with country folk in the hungry, old days, and the eggs are easily predated by crows, magpies and even stoats which are good tree-climbers. More sensitive pigeon men do not care to shoot the birds in the peak nesting times, as the thought of a pair of orphans dying of starvation is not a pleasant one. A close inspection of the crop of a shot bird will show the pulpy excrescence inside the skin which indicates that 'milk' is being made — but by then, of course, it is too late!

A pigeon's loose feathers give it the reputation of carrying shot

A pigeon will sometimes climb steeply from the top of a tree, stall at the highest point and clap its wings together behind its back before swooping down again, either to repeat the process or to land in another tree. This is known as 'cocking' and is a mating display. When courting, a cock will chase a hen from branch to branch, the clap of wings being audible at a great distance. The old Fenman with only one cartridge to spare would wait until two sat together on a twig, preferably in the act of mating, and then fire his single, careful shot, bagging two for the price of one. Very unsporting!

The secret of the pigeon's success lies in its adaptability and the rapid development since the war of intensive arable farming. Once by no means a common bird, the pigeon has been favoured by cereals, brassicas, rape, peas, beans, clover and all the other things it loves and which UK farmers grow all too successfully. The bird has a high metabolic rate and expends a great deal of energy in its arrow-swift powerful flight. It needs to eat in large amounts and eat well to sustain such a workrate and it chooses the best. Peas when seeds or young tender shoots, scattered grain, the delicate buds of fruit trees, the sweetest of newly sprung rape — it picks everything dew-fresh and gourmet selected. It tends to feed in large flocks, and a knowledge of the pigeon flavour of the week is an important weapon in the decoyer's armoury.

The pigeon spends the night in the company of its fellows roosting in a wood or high in a roadside tree. This represents the second opportunity for the sportsman who when he forsakes his decoys, can ambush them either as they fly in from the fields to the roosting wood or within the wood itself as the birds actually drop in to land. A strong wind is favourable for this sort of shooting as the pigeons tend to fly lower and land quickly in the wood to escape a buffeting rather than circling high and wary a number of times to see if the coast is clear.

Pigeon shooting is not easy because the bird is so quick and evasive, having been shot at on and off for the last fifty years or more. There are many old pigeons and a number of stupid pigeons, but rarely one which is both. Let us take a pigeon's eye view of a typical morning's activity, for it is only by knowing the quarry and knowing it well, its preferences, conduct and behaviour patterns, that the serious decoyer may come to terms with it.

You spent the night roosting in an oak wood, undisturbed by shooting as the keeper is keeping the place quiet for his pheasants. You have digested your bulging crop full of the best part of half-a-pint of prime seed wheat and you need to feed again soon. Where you went yesterday seems as good a place as any, for the newly-drilled field was undisturbed and two thousand of you had fed there for most of the day and even then had not cleared the grain scattered by a careless field driller, eager to rush his corn into an ill-prepared seed bed.

With a clatter of wings a cluster of birds leaves from the next tree, climbing over the dewy field below. This activity makes you nervous: other birds leave, stretching out like a long string of beads and all heading in the same direction. Then you

Pigeons eat ivy berries in spring

launch yourself, clap your wings, soar briefly, and set off with quick wingbeats on the path of the others.

The flightline aims for an electricity pylon on the far hill, for you often fly by landmarks, using conspicuous trees or hedges to guide you. You do not care to work too hard for your food, for it is the instinct of any wild creature to match intake with output in terms of energy, but you prefer to feed in the company of others of your species. The flock is a comforting thing, for five hundred pairs of eyes are better protection than one and should a predator strike, the odds on you being the unlucky victim are greatly reduced in a large flock.

As you fly you operate an efficient ground-scanning system, rather like a military aircraft which gives the pilot a display of the terrain before him — but all you have is a pair of the sharpest eyes in the bird kingdom. These scan the ground a hundred yards ahead, identifying potential hazards on the ground. The landscape below you is a patchwork quilt worked in greens and browns with the occasional startling flash of yellow where the oilseed rape is just coming into flower. A tractor crawls back and forth, scoring a serrated, symmetrical pattern of lighter stripes on a late corn drill. Your sharp eyes identify each object, dismissing the safe, reacting to the dangerous.

A farmer leaning on a gate causes you to jink sideways to pass him a good sixty yards wide. Who knows better than the oft shot-at woodpigeon the range of a 12-bore shotgun? A flash of white from an upturned human face has you throwing yourself across the sky, for such pale, unexpected glimpses are often the prelude for a shower of stinging pellets.

Then, below, you see a cluster of grey shapes feeding by the edge of an open field. You lose height, take a cautious circle, cup your wings and fly into the wind on your landing run. Then you become suspicious. Those pigeons look curiously immobile: they are all spaced an equal distance apart and there

26

are pinches of white feathers lying here and there. Something is wrong, and as you flick your wings to jink out of danger, the sun catches the 'pigeons' and you see a quick flash of reflected light, which would not come from a bird with real feathers.

On you go, and half-a-mile further on you see another group of birds, more reassuring this time, standing in clusters of twos and threes, no white feathers, no reflected light and again you spiral down to land among them, looking for an open space towards the rear of the pack, for pigeon etiquette does not permit landing at the front of the queue — like most ground-feeding birds, pigeons usually work upwind. Just as you are making the home run, you catch a movement in the hedge bottom, a flicker of white as a human face peers over a netting hide, the briefest glimpse of a menacing, black gun-barrel waved aloft.

Like lightning you throw yourself across the sky and away: there is a double bang and you hear the hiss of pellets, red-hot needles streaking past underneath you, but by now you are out of range and safely away. A basic error on the part of two separate pigeon decoyers has saved your life.

You are not unduly alarmed, for hardly a day passes without an encounter with an artificial decoy 'picture' or the sound of a shot — such things are part of your life and while you know they are to be avoided, you do not fear death, for it is a concept of which you can have no comprehension.

A one in ten thousand mutant: a white woodpigeon shot by the author

At last you find the real thing: a group of twenty birds and as you scan for danger, you notice a flicker of white on a wing as another bird lands in the group. In a hedgerow ash sits a cluster of other pigeons and still more are in the air with you and trickling in to land. All appears to be in order, and there is a tempting landing area just right for you, so you jam on the air brakes and, still wary of unexpected danger, you land lightly on the open space below.

It may be that that was your last move and that a truly expert decoyer had used lofters and flappers to deceive even you. However, it would be a pity to kill you off so early in your career as a woodpigeon, so we will assume that all was well and you were able to eat your fill undisturbed. You walk here and there in short, busy steps, a peck here, two pecks somewhere else, trying to keep head to wind for most of the time, for a wind from your back ruffles your feathers, cools your body and makes you feel generally uncomfortable.

A buzzard flaps over two fields off and suddenly every neck in your flock is upstretched, the white collar now prominent and warning of possible danger. You take no chances and have made sure to leave enough space around you to allow for a sudden departure without the risk of aerial collisions.

Then you are up with a clatter, but the danger passes and after flying in a wide circle, you settle in one of a clump of beech trees on the edge of the meadow. Here you sit for an hour, enjoying the sunshine, digesting and indulging in a little desultory preening. Then you begin to feel hungry again: a little green salad would go down well after that parching grain. You launch yourself from the tree, into the wind and, one of a flock of eighty birds you arrow across the sky, over the high thorn hedge, well out of gunshot range of the ground and on to a distant field of newly sprouted peas which lies on the far side of the hill. Your automatic radar is switched on and you see nothing below to alarm you.

End of romance, and of course no human can ever know exactly what it feels like to be a woodpigeon, but if you are to be a successful pigeon shooter you must at least attempt the exercise. 'Know your quarry' is the essential rule for any hunter and the pigeon decoyer is no exception. As Coats says: 'Learn to think like a pigeon.'

Muzzle loaders can be used . . .

2 · The Hardware

This ought to be the shortest chapter ever written, for any shotgun will do for pigeon shooting. There is no special specification for a pigeon gun as there is for, say, a wildfowling gun. Some elderly weapons marked or described in auction catalogues as 'Pigeon Gun' were designed for shooting live pigeons from traps in competition shooting before the development of clay pigeon shooting. Such guns are usually heavy and have long barrels, but do not be deceived by the name into believing that here is the weapon for ambushing the grey hordes when they come in to the peas.

So, any old gun, even a Pigeon Gun will do, but of course life is never quite that simple and a few qualifications and some of my personal prejudices might be helpful. Firstly, while a single-barrelled gun is perfectly efficient and will certainly kill pigeons, its very design imposes limitations. Pigeons often come to decoys in groups of more than one, and the big bags are made up by a high proportion of right-and-lefts or double shots. The single gun is therefore at an obvious disadvantage, but if this is the only gun you have, then use it by all means. Most single-barrelled shotguns are fully choked and this is an unsuitable boring for a decoy gun, so he who persists with the single must have most of the choke removed.

The same might be said of the semi-automatic, and unless it has a choice of screw-in chokes, the choke must be eased considerably before the gun becomes suitable for hide work. I have revised my opinions of the semi-auto since I wrote *Modern Pigeon Shooting* and now believe that it is perfectly acceptable as a practical weapon. The old 'pro' pigeon men of my youth used nothing else but the Browning 5-shot auto; it was standard equipment and I have seen it used to deadly effect. One of the 'old boys' gave his Browning such heavy and regular use that one day it literally fell to pieces, completely worn out by a degree of honest wear and tear which ten normal guns in ten shooting lifetimes might have expected.

My personal prejudice comes about because I am a left-handed shot, so that with a normal semi-auto the empty case and waste gases shoot out across my face each time I fire. I believe that most models may now be had in a left-handed version. Breda, Browning and Franchi are all well and soundly made and will do well for pigeon shooting. Unsporting, you say? There are no unsporting guns, only unsporting people. The Wildlife and Countryside Act (1981) restricts to three the number of cartridges which may be loaded into the weapon at any one time.

Most pigeon shooters use a standard double-barrelled game gun, either over-and-under or side-by-side. The OU is probably the more widely used of the two due to the easy availability and reasonable price of imported models as well as the fact that the OU is favourite for clays and may also be used for game shooting so that one gun will serve all purposes. It is also a matter of fashion and there can be little doubt that five times as many OU guns as side-by-sides are sold today.

The old criticism of the OU in a hide was the minor one that the gun needs a long drop of the barrels for loading and in a cramped hide this calls for a little care. Nothing is more annoying than lifting your barrels at a likely bird and getting the foresight inextricably tangled in the netting, so that you find yourself involved in a frenzied *danse macabre* with six yards of camouflage while the birds flee in panic.

The side-by-side has a shallower drop, may be more easily had with short barrels, tends to be lighter in weight and, I have found, rather more handy than its popular cousin.

The trick is to use a gun which suits you and with which you feel at home, be it a muzzle-loader or double-barrelled 8-bore: no joke, for I have used both from a pigeon hide; the latter was completely hopeless, but I did manage to knock down a bird or two with the former.

As for bore, a 12-bore tends to be standard, but there are more 20-bores to be seen in the shooting field generally, especially since perceptive importers such as Gunmark started bringing in some beautifully made 20-bores, the Beretta and the Viscount being cases in point. The Browning Citori 20-bore is another beauty of which I have some first-hand knowledge. The 16-bore: fine, but ammunition is not so easily available and this less common weapon is seen more on the continent than here. The .410 is not really up to the job but I have little time for this gun in any circumstances and do everything I can to discourage the myth that this is the gun to start a boy on his shooting career: nothing could be further from the truth. A 20-bore is better in every way.

As for borings, the whole secret of shooting well lies in *range*

Patterns: full choke — bad; half choke — better; improved cylinder — best

and thus by implication in the dual philosopher's stone of open borings and small shot. If he is any good, a pigeon decoyer relies on bringing the birds over his decoy pattern so that they present easy shots at close range, rarely more than twenty-five yards away and often less than that. Not for him the forty yarder flashing past, startled and alert, far beyond his decoys. Thus, for a vast majority of shots taken at close range, open bores will allow the pattern to develop early and be well spread at even a short distance. Tight choke means close patterns and birds either missed clean or blown to smithereens.

I know some pigeon men who swear by open cylinder (ie no choke whatever) in both barrels, and their results are certainly impressive. This might be a little extreme for most of us, so a reasonable compromise for a double gun might be improved cylinder and either quarter or half choke, for a second shot at a fleeing pigeon might well be taken at rather longer range than the first, easy chance at an unsuspecting target. For a single barrel, pump action or semi-auto, improved cylinder or skeet-boring will serve nicely. Improved cylinder allows a 25% aiming error at thirty yards (27m) over full choke, a useful statistic which speaks for itself. We pigeon men often need all the help we can get!

Another old myth is perpetuated by hoary old pigeon men who remark laconically that a pigeon can 'carry the shot', by which they mean be hard hit by pellets and still escape. Nonsense! This myth has arisen because of the dense feathering on the bird, especially over the rump. What is more, these feathers are white and therefore very conspicuous when they become detached from their owner. Add to that the fact that most missed or 'pricked' birds are missed behind, below or both and you have the explanation. It needs only one pellet from the leading edge of the pattern to rake through that thick quilt of loose feathers and a great cloud of them flies out and drifts downwind.

The shooter imagines that such a show indicates a bird fairly peppered and he watches eagerly, expecting to see it drop at any moment. The fact that often it fails to do so gives rise to the theory that pigeons can 'carry the shot'. Having said as much, a pigeon shooter is wise to watch a hit bird out of sight, for quite often he is rewarded by the sight of it tumbling down dead a field and a half away. Sometimes a hit bird will settle in a fieldside tree. This bird should be left; walk towards it to administer the coup-de-grace and it will fly again long before you are in range and probably be lost. Stay where you are and within half-an-hour the bird will generally fall dead from the branch.

We do our old-timer a minor injustice, perhaps, for the pigeon is doubtless a tough bird, streamlined, with close-knit feathers on its breast and dense, muscular flesh. When fully gorged with dry peas or acorns, the distended bulge of the crop acts as a shield from the front, and there are certainly attested cases of this tightly-packed, wobbly chainmail deflecting the pellets, from even quite close range. Similarly when fleeing, the bird presents a target of the well padded rump already mentioned.

However, but for these isolated cases, a pigeon will fall dead if fairly caught in the centre of your pattern. The trick is quite simply to use small shot and shoot straight, a maxim for all forms of field shooting and if you can do this, you will, in a single morning, dispel the 'carrying the shot' legend.

This leads us to cartridges, and here again the pigeon man need not be fussy when it comes to brand name, but he does need the right shot size. The old custom was to settle for fives on the theory that a pigeon was hard to kill, but I greatly prefer sixes or sevens. The smaller size gives you more pellets to the ounce and I have explained already that good shooting is all about patterns. Sevens present a denser pattern for the same spread as fives: they have better penetration, most gun shops stock them as opposed to the now less fashionable fives and I have found them excellent also for other forms of shooting from duck and pheasant to snipe and sporting clays.

The cartridge market is a competitive one and many imported brands from America or the continent are well-produced and can hold up their heads even when compared with our own brands. Time was when this claim could not be made, and some cheap, imported cartridges were full of surprises, one going off with a mighty bang and heavy recoil, the next merely giving an extended phutt and squirt of sparks because, for some reason, the shot had been left out. Those days have gone and the buyer may shop around for the ones which best

Continental ammunition used to be unpredictable

suit his pocket, entirely confident that they will serve him satisfactorily.

If you can afford to buy in quantities of five thousand or more you may expect a healthy discount. Some pigeon men form little consortia to buy a huge number and thus share the discount. Home-loading was once popular, especially when a team of friends shared a machine and bought the components in bulk. However, the cost of the ingredients has increased as the price of ready-made ammunition has gone down and home-loading is now more an operation for the specialist who wishes to custom-load cartridges for some specific purpose.

Modern cartridges have highly sophisticated wadding systems, with plaswads of various specifications making it possible to develop a pattern early or to hold it together for longer — in other words taking over the role of choke in the muzzles of the gun. If you are uncertain, your gunsmith will advise you on the interpretation of the runes on the side of the box. The pigeon man should not have much cause for concern, as specialist wadding is more usual in clay pigeon ammunition. The field pigeon shooter will go for standard game loads, $1^{1}/_{16}$oz (30g) being a good all-round load, although my personal preference is for the 1oz load.

What is important is to match the cartridge to the gun and this can be checked easily by means of a pattern plate. This is a heavy steel square propped up safely against a straw stack or the like. Paint it with whitewash, aim at the middle of it from a measured thirty yards (27m) — within which, remember, you expect to take most of your shots — and fire. The spread of the pattern will easily be seen, and if you make a cardboard cut-out of a flying pigeon (easily done from a dead bird) you can see if it will fit in any gaps without being touched. A *minimum* of two pellets in vital spots should be considered necessary. As different chokes in various guns produce patterns which vary with different brands of cartridge, try a range of brands, having a few shots with each to be certain you did not pick a fluke, and find out which one gives the best results.

By and large, the best advice is to use a gun with which you feel comfortable, stick to it and do not do as some do and change at least once a season, for that way confusion and inconsistency lie. Buy cartridges as cheaply as you can, but half-an-hour testing the pattern, just to make sure, is time well spent.

Thus, the Humphreys formula for bag-filling shooting which works as well for pigeons as for all game, is as follows:

1 Open borings
2 Small shot
3 Close range
4 Short barrels (this is a purely personal preference)
5 Light gun

Getting the birds to come within close range is what the art of pigeon decoying is all about and therein lies the fieldcraft which marks an expert from a novice. Anyone can fire hopefully at a scared bird and knock it down at extreme range with a fluke pellet in the head. He will not do it often, and if such is his general approach to shooting he will not last long. The long-range expert who boasts of his regular and prodigious 'fifty yarders' is a blemish on the sport of shooting.

Equipment should be as lightweight as possible

3 · Bits and Pieces

Hide, hide poles, decoys and netting are tools of the trade of the pigeon man and they will be dealt with fully in later chapters, but there are many useful accessories, some more important than others but few of them essential, which will help make his life a trifle more easy.

Something to cut and snick away the brambles is high on the list and it is hard to imagine how the decoyer can construct a hedge-bottom hide without one. One tough bramble curling across your face or a frond of willow in just the wrong place is enough to ruin your day, and just try breaking it with your bare hands — quite impossible. Secateurs are light, easy to pack and quite good enough to remove such nuisances. A straight slasher is heavier but will do for the light twigs as well as more substantial branches, but of course it should not be used on hardwood saplings unless you have no wish to be invited again. Machete, short-handled billhook — I have seen them all used, but go for lightness, strength and a razor-sharp edge. My own preference is for the straight-handled slasher which I call 'the pigeon shooter's friend'.

Binoculars are also handy, but few families can afford two pairs, one for pigeon shooting and the other for family birdwatching outings or trips to the seaside. However, as an aid for scanning a feeding field or following what you suspect might be the start of a flightline, binoculars can be extremely useful. As with most of your equipment, go for light weight and small size for you may have to carry it a considerable distance. Perfect are those miniature, folding binoculars which are now readily available and cost £60 or so. These fit into a breast pocket and are featherlight, better for your purpose than the ex-German U-boat captain's glasses which resemble two milk bottles and weigh in at 6lb (2.7kg), which you bought in a rash moment from a small ad in the paper. For all-round field-work for sporting and leisure occasions, 7 x 50 (ie a magnification of x7 and an object lens measuring 50mm) are best. The large object lens gathers the light efficiently and this is useful at dawn and dusk when the sportsman is often out and about.

You need not be an aged pensioner and nor is it a sign of weakness to require a seat. A man seated in a hide has a greater field of sky against which to see approaching birds, he needs a smaller hide than a standing man and to be on your feet throughout a long day's decoying is a form of masochism I can well do without.

Several patent, shortened shooting sticks are available and these collapse in various ways to make them less bulky, but they are not comfortable enough for a long wait, and unless the footplate has been especially enlarged, they tend to sink slowly into ground which is anything less than iron hard.

Shooting sticks should have wide plates for soft ground

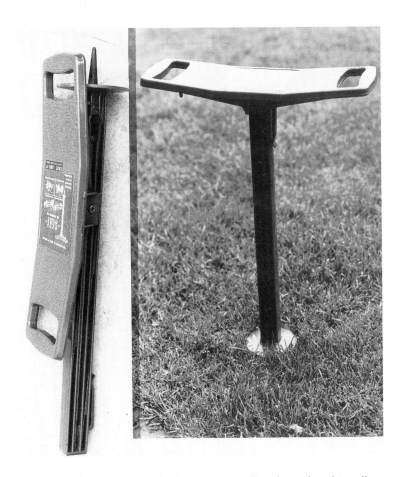

Some sort of seat is essential. Many use a 5-gallon drum, but this collapsible seatstick is light and comfortable

No pigeon man cares to spend money unless it is absolutely necessary, but prefers to make do, mend and improvise — an inventive streak is an essential attribute for the decoyer. For a seat he will use a five-gallon metal oil or chemical drum, the rim hammered flat, and a cushion of coarse sacking placed carefully to protect his nether regions. Really wily old experts have produced a removable lid or flap so that items such as hide netting, lunch or a few spare decoys may be carried inside. The seat is carried slung on the shoulder by means of a piece of cord and, for all its bulkiness, it has little weight; lugging it along to the far end of the field is amply rewarded by the comfort and stability it provides thereafter.

Your gun should be carried in a gun-slip which allows you to sling it on your back leaving the hands free; this also protects the weapon from scratches and scrapes as you struggle over barbed wire or force a track through the thorns. It has been said, and I have said it too, that a pigeon hide is no place for a 'best' London gun, but after all, I do not see why not. Much of the pleasure in owning such a handsome and valuable thing lies in using it, so I can see little point in shooting many pigeons with a £50 gun while you have at home a Boss or Purdey you are scared stiff of using. A good leather gun-slip will protect it from many potential hazards. Brettonbank Fieldsports make a superb quality hide-leather slip, Brady make a top class canvas one, while plastic ones lined with nylon fur may be bought anywhere; it will always be money well spent.

All those cartridges of which I spoke earlier will have to be carried, probably the single most heavy item you will have to handle. Take a good lot and do not risk running out: either you bring the cartridges home again or you have the weight of dead pigeons instead, and remember that a hundred pigeons weigh almost exactly a hundredweight. Leave a carton of 250 as spares in the boot of your car so that in the event of a day of a lifetime developing you will be able to nip back during a lull and collect some reserve stocks. For instant use, cartridges may be carried in a belt or in your side pockets; although the belt certainly distributes the weight evenly, I find the pocket more accessible, but be careful not to mix packets of Polos or those cylindrical cigarette lighters in the same pocket. Also remember that a 20-bore cartridge dropped into a 12-bore breech can have disastrous effects when a fresh 12-bore cartridge is fired on top of it. Take 150 cartridges to the hide with you, 50 in your belt and pockets, the rest in their cartons in the rucksack.

We all have our favourite type of bag for pigeon shooting and in my time I have tried most of them. Long-time favourite was an old-style frame rucksack large enough to take everything in one go and with some handy pockets for the bits and pieces. The beauty of this type of bag is that you can carry great

(above) *Fully laden: balance your load and leave the hands free;* (below left) *A sack is a good means of carrying shot birds;* (right) *The net decoy sack will take more than enough decoys*

weights economically and still leave both hands free for gun, poles and negotiating obstacles.

For those who prefer the more traditional shoulder bag the usual net-fronted game bag will do, but mostly they are far too small. Far better is the postman's delivery satchel type of bag, upon which is closely modelled the cavernous 'Bag for all Seasons', rubber-lined and made in stout green canvas by Shooting Developments and available from many good gun shops. This bag will carry an enormous amount of equipment and almost innumerable dead pigeons.

For those who use large numbers of artificial decoys, the decoy-carrying net bag is ideal, made from strong nylon with two carrying straps so that it can be carried on the shoulders like a rucksack. This will hold a great many decoys which are light but also bulky and thus awkward to carry in other ways. I have found one slight drawback with this bag — very few things are perfect in this life — which is that those decoys with sharp beaks, metal pegs or hooks on the tails for hanging them up, do tend to become caught in the meshes, and taking them out becomes a matter for much blasphemy and a raising of the blood pressure. If you do not use that type of decoy, the bag is nothing but excellent. It is available from many gun shops and mail order firms.

A good penknife is essential and, of course, no countryman would venture out without one — as soon forget his trousers — and I need not take up space in explaining the many uses to which it may be put, from gutting rabbits to carving cheese, but not both in the same operation — at least not before wiping it swiftly on the trouser leg. The Swiss army knife which is advertised as more of a mobile workshop than a common 'shut-knife' is spoken of very highly by those who can afford one. Sadly, I am not in their ranks.

A primitive first-aid kit is also useful: you may use it only once in a season, but on that occasion it will prove a godsend. A cut finger which bleeds over everything, your gun included (and blood is a mighty ruster of gunmetal), can be more than a nuisance and can be so easily remedied by a piece of sticking plaster.

Add some of this list to your nets, poles and decoys and you will realise how important it is for the decoyer to plan his load carefully and organise exactly how he intends to carry it. The pigeon man tends to travel unnecessarily heavily and takes with him so many non-essential 'just in case' items that he can grow to resemble as much a beast of burden as a sportsman.

Some recognise the risk and have devised a type of war waggon, a cross between a porter's barrow and a golf trolley on which the shooter piles all his equipment. The waggon is light enough to be lifted over fences and ditches while its comfortably sprung pram wheels will take it over quite rough going, as long as it is not too wet and muddy. I leave dispirited but compulsive equipment collectors with that thought.

The pigeon man often takes too much gear

All you need to shoot a pigeon is a gun and a cartridge. Start with that premise and work up from there. Decoys and hide-making equipment, in that order of importance, will be necessary sooner or later and I suppose you do need a bag in which to carry it all, but really you can get away with little else. Ken Gandy of Ely is and was a great pigeon shooter who taught me much about the sport. He killed many thousands of birds using half-a-dozen decoys and as much equipment as he could cram into an ex-WD gas-mask bag. He had not made the mistake which many make now, namely that good equipment and lots of it equals large bags of birds. There is no short cut to fieldcraft and skill and the best gear in the world will not make a bungler into an expert. Of this — more later.

As for clothing, there are a hundred clothing shops in your neighbourhood eager to sell you this or that waterproof marvel with stormproof collar and cuffs, full-length zip, especially warm lining and pop-over hood with the special camouflage finish. As with guns and cartridges, sporting clothing is another buyer's market with a generally high standard of design and material available.

For cold winds or rain the waxproofed cloth coat by Barbour or the equivalent is well proven, but you need a pair of waterproof trousers to go with it, otherwise the

The human face is a great bird frightener

rain runs off the coat and soaks your legs. At other times this apparel is too warm and you need a light, camouflaged top coat in greys or greens to complete the ensemble, a shirt that is *not* white and a hat with a brim. Remember, this is a pigeon shoot, not a fashion parade and the whole idea is that the pigeons are not supposed to see you, much less admire your sartorial elegance.

Pigeons are scared by sudden flashes of white such as are caused by a human face suddenly upturned or human hands spasmodically flourished. Hide-discipline will teach you to sit still, but a wide-brimmed floppy bush hat will allow you to peep up beneath the edge without raising your head. Mittens will help conceal hand movements, rather warm on a hot day but not much of a sacrifice to make for a heavier bag and fewer frightened pigeons.

You will find that very often, the background offered by the countryside where you intend to build your hide tends to be of a lighter rather than a darker hue. Never thought about it? Go on, look out of the window or if you are in town do it next time you are near a field boundary hedge. The majority of colours for most times of the year are provided by pale, faded grass, bleached rushes, elder-flowers, fawn stalks of corn and almost white dead twigs, the only dark hues being the knotty trunks of hawthorn. Many quite mature trees have barks which are lichen grey-green rather than black or chocolate brown which is the colour of many waterproof shooting coats.

The criteria are warmth, comfort, freedom of movement to swing the gun and of a colour, or blend of colours, which match the general background of the sort of places you do most of your shooting.

There is certainly a cult fostered by commercial interests in many field sports which pressurises the sportsman to festoon himself with every conceivable useless piece of gadgetry. An old pigeon man from 'the sticks' once came up to town and visited a famous gun shop. After staring round for some minutes at the Aladdin's cave of accessories, he remarked laconically, 'I never knew there were so many things a man could do without!'

Part of the point of pigeon shooting is that you need very little specialist equipment and that generally any old thing will do, with the possible exception of the decoys and hide-making equipment. It is a sport which relies on resourcefulness, fieldcraft, a knowledge of the quarry and a sense of individualism. In some ways it is like wildfowling and attracts the old-fashioned genuine sportsman, the man likely to go ferreting when he cannot go pigeon shooting, or clay shooting when he can do neither.

4 · Decoys

Recalling the pigeon's eye view of the world described earlier, we remember that the pigeon is a gregarious bird, fond of the company of its fellows. It is this characteristic which the decoyer seeks to exploit: if he can present passing birds with what appears to be a flock of their feeding brethren down below, a flock which is in a likely place and which closely resembles the real thing, if he persuades them to alight then he has succeeded. The dual pulls of greed and the desire for companionship will bring the newcomers in to join the feast.

Obviously the more realistic the picture, the more confident the real birds will be. If the decoys look wrong, are striking unpigeon-like attitudes or are in groupings which look unnatural, wild pigeons will smell a rat and leave the scene as quickly as possible. While this is usually the case, pigeons can sometimes behave foolishly for such wary birds. Once I shot seventy-six using a squad of crude home-made decoys which were all I had in the car at the time. They were made from sections of grey, plastic guttering, roughly cut to shape and daubed black and white in more or less the right places. Once in position they shone hideously, throwing back the spring sunlight with a hard glitter. I was on the point of gathering them in when a single pigeon came, paid the price for his curiosity, and was followed by another, then a third, then half-a-dozen.

I set up the dead birds on wires and a steady trickle followed, coming with such confidence that I did not need to leave my hide again until they stopped at tea-time and I found I had made a good bag. This is an exception to the rule and for ninety-nine times out of a hundred, any self-respecting pigeon would steer well clear of such monstrosities.

Decoying originated with the attracting of duck, geese and plover to the shooter's position, but that was an easy challenge compared to drawing the oft shot-at and well-educated pigeon of the 1990s.

Clearly, then, the right decoys are the most realistic ones and the one which comes out head and shoulders above the rest is the dead bird. If you are out regularly, it is no problem to keep back a dozen or so dead pigeons, preferably clean and neat ones, and lie them in a tidy row on a garage floor to cool in natural postures. Those who shoot less often may keep a supply of shot birds in the deep freeze. It is not good enough simply to fill a polythene bag and then drop it in, for the birds will freeze in hideous, nightmarish postures which no human force will change until they have thawed out. Lie them in a row on their backs, heads hanging down through a wire grill and next morning they will be in natural shape and ready for action. Buying fresh birds for decoys is rather a desperate measure and very much a last resort — most decoyers I know are better at selling pigeons than buying them.

Like all decoys, dead pigeons should be set up *more or less* facing the wind, but not all standing at precisely the same angle like a file of guardsmen on parade. Some are sideways to the wind, an odd one may even have his back to it, so use your observation of the real thing to help you present a natural picture.

Hedgerow twigs will do to mount dead birds

The pigeon may be laid on its tummy on the ground in a place where it will not be hidden by fronds of vegetation. Stroke its feathers down neatly, fan its tail a little so that it looks plump and attractive and remove any of the white feathers which pigeons alive or dead will shed at the drop of a hat. Scattered feathers and birds lying on their backs have an off-putting effect on approaching newcomers.

The position of the head represents an important bone of contention. The old trick was to prop up the head with a piece of 9in galvanised wire pushed into the soft skin of the throat. This stretched the neck to its full height showing the white neck flash clearly. Other decoyers believed that the white collar was displayed as an alarm signal and, not caring to present the real pigeons with a flock in a state of fright, preferred to keep the collar muted and not fully extended.

Here again, observation of the real thing will prove invaluable: in most feeding flocks the majority of the birds will have their heads down filling their faces with the farmer's newly sprouted rape, others will be in the act of walking to the next succulent patch, and one or two will be jittery and might, with extended necks, be peering at some distant object which just could represent danger. This, after all, is how most flock systems operate and why, by and large, they are successful. This mixture is what the dead-bird decoyer must seek to reproduce. I knew a pigeon shooter who went so far as to set the decoys nearest his hide in the wary, neck up, position, on the theory that they were the ones which were most likely to be suspicious.

Push the wire in at the base of the crop, up inside the neck and gently into the cranium from below. This leaves no wire showing, and with the other end stuck into the ground, the decoy may be made to hold its head at any angle. Some decoys

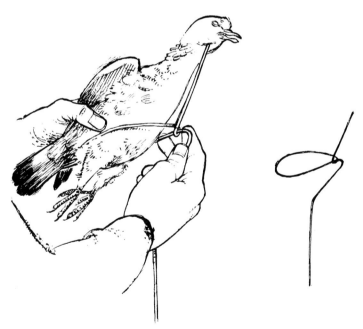

Using a patent cradle for a dead bird

Long canes are useful in standing corn

A sharp stick or wire is useful to support the head of a dead bird decoy

need no wire but may be simply laid down as though in the act of pecking, though try to prevent the head lolling on one side by supporting it on a few crumbs of earth or plant stalks.

Another trick is to push a thin bamboo stick through the dead bird's vent, up through the body and into the head. This is useful where the crop on the field is more than a few inches high and where you wish to ensure that your decoys will be seen above it. If you try this dodge — and few nowadays seem to use it — make sure the stick traverses the bird just inside the backbone, otherwise it will twiddle round and lie on its back the moment you set it in position.

However, the idea behind this messy and rather time-consuming system is sound enough. The best decoys in the world are useless if they cannot be seen easily from above.

Next best thing to the dead bird is a stuffed one. Pigeons may be stuffed by a professional taxidermist but this is far too expensive. It is easy enough to do your own: cut the bird down the breast-bone and peel back the skin, removing breast bone, meat and all the innards. Paint all exposed skin with 50% formaldehyde solution, inject the base of the wings, the head and any fleshy parts with the same preservative, cut off the legs at the hip, and stuff the body cavity with cotton wool or balls of rolled-up newspaper. Insert a length of coat-hanger wire along the length of the bird and finally stitch up the skin with your best Boy Scout needlework over-and-over stitching.

Place the bird to dry carefully, making sure that the wings are neatly furled and the tail spread out in a handsome fan. Remember that in whatever posture you leave a freshly preserved bird, in that posture will it remain until it crumbles to dust. They need careful handling thereafter for they are easily damaged and do not much care to be rained on, so if a shower threatens you must take them in. Transporting them can prove a real headache and on no account should they be jostled in the bottom of a grubby game bag along with secateurs, boxes of cartridges and other bits and pieces. They will not last a couple of outings if so treated. Remember that your aim is for feather-perfect birds and not ghastly caricatures with shed feathers and semi-skeletal appearance.

There is no short cut, they have to be carried in their own special box where they can be cared for en route. A wine or spirits box designed to take a dozen bottles is ideal. First drink the contents, then slip a stuffed bird head down into each compartment. As for carrying the box itself, there is nothing for it but to carry it in your arms, and very awkward it will prove.

I do not use stuffed birds any more, although time was when I used them regularly. The whole thing was just too much bother and while they were effective enough as attractors, the practical problems of making and carrying them called for a less slothful pigeon man than the spokesman of these lines. Also, stuffed decoys tend to lose their natural feather gloss after a time and grow rather dark in colour so that regular replacements are called for. A final word of advice for those who decide to try the home-stuffed birds: watch out for the formaldehyde and wear rubber gloves when using it. It is also nasty stuff to inhale.

A compromise is to preserve the wings only of real pigeons and fix them to polymer, full-bodied decoys. Cut off the wing, inject the flesh end with the formaldehyde, pin the wing onto a board to ensure that it sets in a realistic shape and, when dry, glue it in position with Araldite or fix it on with Velcro. The wing may be preserved in the closed or open position, for a pair of spread wings can often prove attractive with their flash of white and easy visibility.

Some fanatics glue sets of feathers onto decoys and I have seen some wonderful examples of painstaking work. I might, at a pinch, be able to envisage myself sticking, laboriously, a set of tail feathers or even primaries in position, one at a time. However, not for a king's ransom would I even contemplate trying the myriad little white ones. The combination of a pot of glue, a hint of a draught and a table covered with loose pigeon feathers is a prospect too hideous to contemplate. Freely and without prejudice I make this option available to the really dedicated pigeon decoyer.

These and many of the other dodges are part of the philosophy of pigeon shooting, for it is a sport which favours the inventive. The best pigeon men are forever trying out new dodges and passing long nights out in garden sheds and workshops hammering away at increasingly complex new inventions which, one day, just might work.

So much for the dead bird and its closest imitators, but having made a strong case for placing it at number one, there are actually some imitations which run it a close second and the best of these will, in one vital respect, beat it. I refer to the factor of *movement*, an element so important in many field sports from the vibrant flicker of a salmon fly to the involuntary flick of gun barrels in the evening sun which turns away the incoming duck. An artificial decoy can, by means of various ingenious springs, wobblers or springy pegs, be made to bob and move in the wind. Again I return to the importance of realism in the picture, and when has the observer seen a flock of pigeons standing stock still except when highly suspicious? A flock feeding and at ease will be constantly on the move, each bird bobbing, pecking, walking quickly to a new place and sometimes fluttering a few yards to a more prolific patch of ground. Stuffed or dead birds cannot be made to behave thus, although by setting the birds slightly sideways to the wind, it is possible to cause the tips of the feathers to flutter slightly which, while it may not convey an impression of animated movement, is better than nothing.

The best modern decoy for movement is the Shell variety, the original lightweight version of which is made by Shooting Developments, and this has proved extremely popular. The trick of the Shell is that it incorporates the essential recognition features of a feeding bird. The overall colour is right and matt finished, the tail is black and the white recognition flashes are boldly depicted, though in the hand it might not resemble the full-bodied bird. Once the unnecessary elements such as legs and underside have been removed — no matter as they are invisible from the air — the hollowed-out shape may be fitted with a peg and clip which fits neatly through the point of balance and the Shell is then suspended, as it were, from one spot and the smallest breeze will cause it to bob up and down in a realistic feeding manner. These decoys are so lightweight that the tiniest whisper of moving air will set them rocking back and forth.

Another advantage is that one fits inside another for carrying so that a score or so may be held in one hand while an almost unlimited number will fit a 'Bag for all Seasons'. Setting them out is a knack easily mastered, but you must remember to collect the pegs at the end of the day for they are easily lost.

Shooting Developments will supply fresh pegs and even separate patent clips. Care must be taken when setting up any Shell decoy to see that the body of the bird and thus its movement is not impeded by any stalks of grass or stubble — these must be pulled up or bent out of the way.

It is also important that the white dowel peg is pushed deeply enough into the ground to hide it from the view of incoming pigeons. Would that the makers dyed the pegs green or dark brown (a job done easily enough at home) so that this problem could be resolved at source.

The other Shell which is popular is precisely the same pattern but made of polymer, the feathers more heavily etched and, in the very latest version, with the addition of a beak. These are heavier than the Shooting Developments' version but they have many of its advantages. A rocker in the form of a springy metal Z-spring gives a most lifelike movement in a wind. The end of the spring fits into the hole in the middle of the back of the decoy where the peg would usu-

Shell decoys on rocking pegs clustered on drilled barley

The polymer feeding decoy — more attractive than the head-up version

ally fit. This type of rocking peg allows the decoy to be positioned above a low stubble or rape crop.

There are various other types of patent cut-outs, silhouettes, and this and that which are fairly useless in these days of pigeons which are nobody's fool, although in the old, easy days they might have worked well enough. If nothing else, they go to prove my theory of the inventive decoyer who would try sections of grey guttering, papier-mâché models (brilliant in a downpour!) or any other medium which might strike his fertile imagination as a possible decoy-making medium. It is, in some ways, a sad thing that the cheapness, general excellence and easy availability of modern, manufactured decoys has removed much of the old incentive to try new ideas.

Also very popular is the full-bodied polymer decoy. This material will not rot, is rainproof, reasonably lightweight but rather bulky and is just right for being carried in the decoy sack already described. This is a full replica of a real woodpigeon with etched feathers, a rough, non-reflective finish and a hole in the middle of the belly to take the mounting stick, and here again it does not take much ingenuity to fashion a rocking peg from a length of old hacksaw blade or similar strip of highly tensile steel.

This decoy is very popular, available in most gun shops and cheap to buy, and you might expect a small discount on a bulk purchase. Two models are available, the head in the normal semi-upright position, or with the head down in a natural feeding posture. The proper name for these decoys is Sportplast and they are made in Italy. Many decoyers use this model exclusively and buy them by the score and in one case by the hundred.

Another first-class full-bodied decoy is the HH inflatable. These decoys have an interesting history for they were the invention of David Home Gall, a great pigeon shooter and maker of his own equipment. Never mass produced, they nonetheless came onto the market in a steady trickle for they were, and still are, made by a one-man business on a cottage industry principle. The patent has changed hands once or twice and is now owned by David Morrison of Wrestlingworth in Bedfordshire who is still turning them out.

The highly rated HH decoy

Full-bodied and made of a soft, rubber skin, this is one of the most realistic artificial decoys in existence, so much so that more than once I have actually shot one of mine both on the ground and when used as a lofter, thinking that a real bird had sneaked in and landed when I was not paying attention. A toy balloon is inflated within the body cavity of the decoy and this gives it a nice fat shape, while the patent, two-pronged peg allows it to be jabbed into the ground. In a stiff breeze it will bob back and forth quite effectively, but its real strength is in its realism.

When deflated a great many may be carried with ease for they crumple up as easily as a handkerchief. Being rubber they are perishable and should not be left squashed in the bottom of a bag but taken out and left in a row on a shelf, out of direct sunlight. Now and then a light dusting inside with French chalk will help to extend their working life, a precaution well worth taking for they are quite expensive. On the credit side you need only a few of them to start you off, no more than ten, certainly, for when properly deployed they present a very natural picture.

The HH decoy is good for lofting — being so light it can be made to perch on quite flimsy twigs on the outside of trees. In time when they become old and tatty, the balloon oozes out through the perished holes like hideous goitres, but all is not lost. Stuff the decoy with scraps of rubber or plastic foam: this removes their collapsible facility, but they are given a new lease of life. Another idea is to fill them with the expanding polystyrene foam used for cavity wall insulation and available in some places in aerosol cans. I am looking out for my next neighbour to have his walls filled so that I can rush round with my HH decoys and beg a few squirts from the nozzle.

The final decoy worth bringing to the attention of readers is the Worldwide Arms pigeon decoy, the Swift. This combines many of the features of the other decoys — deep shell pattern, mounted on a patent rocking peg and with an unusual vane above the tail which ensures that the decoy faces the wind. The bird is of larger than life-size, reasonably priced and, at the time of writing, brand-new on the market. I have not tried them in any numbers, but I have heard favourable comments from those who have. I believe that Worldwide Arms has invested heavily

New on the market, the Swift decoy

in the manufacturing process for this model, so it is likely to be with us for a few years to come.

Pay your money and take your choice. If I cannot lay my hands on dead birds, I use a mixture of artificials, predominantly Shooting Development Shells with a few Sportplast full-bodied decoys scattered amongst them and indeed, any other odd ones I have by me. Ever an optimist, I believe that with a variety, there must be something there which will strike a chord of recognition in the pigeons and I resolutely ignore those who try to tell me that there is just as likely to be something in my mixture to scare them stiff.

Another useful dodge is to use a crow or feral pigeon as a 'confidence' decoy somewhere in your pattern. Again, your observation of the real thing will show you that very often a crow, gull, pheasant or some other conspicuous bird will be feeding near a flock of pigeons. Your aim is to present a realistic scene which the birds would expect to see, so the extra decoy scores on that count, but it also acts as an eye-catcher, most useful when you are decoying over a thick crop and are worried about the visibility of your static decoys. The wildfowlers of old knew this well enough, and they would use a white duck in with their decoys for the same purpose. The fact that it was a strident quacker helped the illusion.

Before leaving the subject of static decoys I must doff my pigeon-shooter's hat to the old, carved wooden decoys. Before rubber or plastic were used, the only decoys available were solid carved wooden ones, finished by hand, carefully painted and standing in a row on a high shelf in the gun shop. They are useless for modern decoying for they weigh a ton, were usually painted too dark and they shine in the feeblest ray of sunlight or drop of rain.

Now they are collectors' pieces, keenly sought after by connoisseurs so if you have one, hang on to it. There must be several left in sheds and attics and I like them because they represent an early form of the sport and a great deal of thought and not a little love went into their manufacture. Some of them were made with movable heads and wings so that the decoyer could present them in any way which took his fancy.

Some early wooden pigeon decoys were ingenious and lovingly made

A squad of mixed decoys creates a realistic picture

No excuse for reiterating that you are after realism and the decoyer who makes his decoys look like the real thing, either by the way he presents them or by the natural look of the decoy itself, will at least be giving himself a fair chance. I suppose the real test is whether your decoys will fool a hawk, a bird with eyes every bit as sharp as a woodpigeon. The Letters page of *Shooting Times* regularly features reports from pigeon shooters whose decoys were carried off by birds of prey. Many species are involved including buzzard, hen harrier, sparrow hawk and even a rough-legged buzzard. Sometimes a decoy is struck and actually carried some distance before the raptor realises its mistake. If you can fool a sparrow hawk you ought to be able to fool a pigeon, so if a bird of prey carries off one of your decoys, regard it as a graceful compliment.

*Some wing flappers
are very ingenious*

5 · Flapping and Lofting

The static decoys described in the previous chapter are the
bread and butter of the pigeon decoyer, for it is with them that
he presents his picture of deception and draws the real pigeons
towards his hide. However, this rather immobile scene, quite
static apart from the bobbing of the Shell decoys on their rocking pegs, may be enhanced in two ways: firstly by the use of a
wing-flapping decoy, secondly by the use of decoys perched
high in a tree.

The idea behind both these ruses is firstly to present a realistic picture, but then more importantly, to provide the eye-
catching feature which will draw birds from a greater distance,
especially when the static decoys do not show up too well.
Very often there will be pigeons sitting in fieldside trees while
the main flock is busy feeding down below. Newcomers will
sometimes settle in such trees before flying down to join the
throng — this is the bird's suspicious nature giving itself a
chance for a leisurely look round before committing itself.
Also, and this is a more common factor now than twenty years
ago, pigeons tend to feed more irregularly and spasmodically
and often spend some prime feeding time just loafing about in
trees, digesting and enjoying the sunshine. This is particularly

true in the long summer days: in winter pigeons are more likely to feed during most of the daylight hours.

Thus a decoy in a tree is seen from a distance and conveys a sense that all is well; it is, therefore, a strong weapon, the use of which the serious decoyer ought to master. Before we look at the art of lofting in full-blown trees, there is a sub-branch of lofting which ought not to be overlooked and I call this the 'pigeon on the twig' dodge. The theory is that you lift a few decoys well above ground level which will make them con- spicuous in peas and short rape and draw the eyes of real pigeons to your own feeding flock.

Simply drag out of the hedge bottom or woodside a dead, bushy branch left over from some previous hedge-trimming operation; when laid on its side the top should be about three feet from the ground. Then you perch about four full-bodied decoys, either Sportplast or HH in the spindly, uppermost twigs. Step back a few paces and you will see that this looks very effective and while real pigeons might not act in such a way, you are permitted this departure from verisimilitude sim- ply because it works.

Some years ago a friend and I were decoying on a field of summer peas and I had packed my static decoys into a tiny patch of almost bare ground. Many pigeons passed but simply could not see my decoys and they dropped in elsewhere. I hauled out a craggy and thorny bough of dead hawthorn, set it on the edge of my pattern and perched four HH decoys on top. From then on, every pigeon saw my decoys immediately and dropped in with confidence, and I killed 102 in an hour and a half. By a curious coincidence, my friend, two hundred yards up the hedge who used the same trick, also killed precisely 102 birds, so we came off the field after a short afternoon with 204 pigeons to our credit and all because of the 'pigeon on a twig' ruse.

Other tricks in this category include setting pigeons on the top strand of a wire fence, a place they often use anyway, or perching them on the fence posts. To hang them on the wire you need some sort of counter-balance system with a long rod

Sportplast decoys make good lofters: decoys lofted in bare trees are a useful tactic

and a lead weight or iron bolt fixed onto the bottom of it to prevent the decoy tumbling over. The 'Percher' does this job very well indeed and it will also serve for placing a decoy in a low, leafless bush. Other variations on this theme will present themselves, such as decoys perched on the top of gooseberry bushes (a trick I used regularly when I had the pigeon shooting on a soft fruit farm), on straw bales or anywhere which shows them proudly. Once I shot fifty-six pigeons by setting all my decoys on the top of four giant, round bales and making my hide behind the fifth one.

Pigeons will often sit actually on the bales of a bale hide set in the middle of a field, so when you are using such a hide, it does no harm to set one or two decoys on canes on the edge of the hide itself.

None of this type of mini-lofting calls for any special equipment, but to elevate birds into a tree calls for a set of lofting poles. It is a myth to think that lofters must be set at the very top of some giant of the forest, fifty feet tall. Choose a solitary tree in a hedge, ash or oak are favourites, and mount your bird on a bare twig on the outside edge of the tree. It need not be very high up and rarely more than twenty feet.

For this you need a set of lofting poles which may be fitted together like the sections of a chimney sweep's brush, with the decoy mounted on the top, pushed up the outside of the tree using low branches as guides and supports. Adding a section

Handling long poles in a wind can be tricky

at a time, work the poles up until you have reached a suitable forked twig, hook the decoy over it and slowly withdraw the poles, taking out a section at a time as you bring them down. Should the poles catch the wind or over balance, threatening to fall, on no account resist or you will bend or break them. Let them go and they will fall softly to the ground, whereupon you take them apart and start all over again.

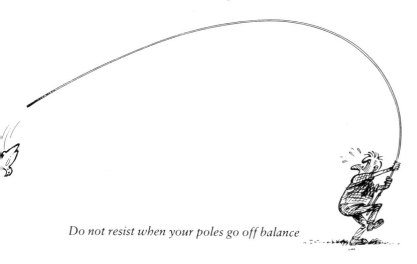

Do not resist when your poles go off balance

The lofted decoy must have a long stick and a counterweight to hold it upright. The stick should hang down from the belly cavity of the bird, and should have a twist of lead near the bottom to hold the decoy steady; it must be thin enough to fit into the open end of the top lofting pole. Lofting is a knack, but it is not all that difficult to master, and those decoyers who complain that it is too much trouble and that the poles are too awkward to carry have missed a rare opportunity which might make the difference between success and failure on a tricky day. Once I killed a very good bag, every bird of which was coming to settle not in my splendid army of ground decoys but in the low ash tree near my hide where I had set three HH lofters. Without the lofters it would have been a very different story.

There are several sets of lofting poles available on the market and I will draw readers' attention to two of them. The first is the type made by Messrs Parsons of Bristol and I believe that

John Storry's combined lofter extension and flapper cradle

this was the first firm to produce this particular accessory. Their poles are of stout aluminium, hollow for lightness and complete with a webbing carrying sling. There is a curved bracket which fits the top section upon which two full-bodied decoys may be placed and the poles left in situ leaning against the tree. I have used Messrs Parsons' equipment for some years with every satisfaction.

The poles are finished in matt olive green and fit together easily, but as with all lofting poles you must be careful to keep earth out of the ends or they will not fit together, and also avoid bending or distorting the poles in any way. Keep the ends lightly coated with grease or candle wax, for nothing is worse than a jammed pole when you have five sections up a tree in a stiff breeze. Each section is six feet (1.8m) long and they are locked together by means of an ingenious push-button system.

Once your decoys are up the tree you will ultimately have the problem of getting them down again. Try fitting the end of the decoy self-righting stick into 1½in (37mm) tube twenty feet up a swaying tree and you will see what I mean. Threading a needle at arm's length in the dark is child's play by comparison. The answer here is simple but ingenious. Buy a large, plastic funnel from the ironmonger's (if you can still find such a place) and fit it to the end of your top pole. A few turns

Shooting Developments lofting poles are ideal

of tape will thicken the nozzle of the funnel to ensure a snug fit. Then it is very like a jet aircraft refuelling in mid-air, for you guide the funnel over the end of the decoy stick and simply lift it off its perch.

The other set of lofting poles which I have used regularly since their recent arrival on the decoying scene are the ones made by Shooting Developments. These have many advantages over the original type, but it is only reasonable to expect that equipment should evolve and improve after many years of field-testing. The S.D. set comes in its own hessian holdall, better than the sling with less risk of the parts getting lost. It also has a shoulder carrying strap.

The pole sections are thinner than usual, but they are incredibly strong. A supplementary set of short sections of the pole allows the decoyer to assemble the set in a great variety of combinations. The real magic is that the poles will also double as hide poles using a set of rods with patent clips which allow them to be fixed at right angles. A supplementary set of pegs and guy ropes are in the holdall for windy days, and two full-bodied Sportplast decoys, complete with self-righting sticks and lead counterweights are available. The sticks fit into the carrying bag with the decoys poking out at the top.

This is a first-class kit, light, adaptable and designed by a practical pigeon shooter with other pigeon shooters in mind. Pigeon shooters tend to be down-to-earth and pragmatic, quick to identify and also to rectify any weakness in their equipment.

You will notice birds of prey taking an interest in your decoys

The S.D. lofting set comes complete with the plastic funnel for taking down the decoys after use.

In my view the lofted decoy is an under-used weapon in the pigeon man's armoury and I urge anyone, from beginner to old hand, to take advantage of it. Like everything else you try, it has its good and bad days the reasons for which are often difficult to guess, but when you use it at the right time in the right place it can be a deadly lure. I have seen a decoyer in action with an excellent hide and a first-class set of decoys: nearby was a solitary tree or a stunted thorn bush, the only one for miles around. Such a site positively cries out for a few lofters which is what the pigeons flighting in would expect to see and which would catch the eye of passing birds and draw them in from a considerable distance.

A final word of caution to the lofting pole man. On no account use your poles in the vicinity of high tension cables. Just touch one by mistake and the poles will prove to be highly efficient conductors of electricity and will kill the decoyer stone dead. Every year it seems, field sportsmen manage to touch overhead cables with fishing rods or lofting poles with fatal results, so please be careful.

Keep your lofting poles well clear of high tension cables

The other supplement to your decoys which is still, I believe, under-used, is the wing-flapping decoy. Does the pigeon shooter's ingenuity know no bounds? He realises the importance of the movement, the one element which I have emphasised in the preceding pages. Even with lofters and some Shell decoys rocking on their pegs, the flash of a grey and white wing is a strong attractor, for pigeons are often flitting here and there or hovering over the flock, while you would expect to see new arrivals all the time. No man-made decoy has yet reproduced this sense of bustle and busy activity but there have been some notable tries.

Some of the inventions have been weird and wonderful. I saw one which worked on a clockwork spring and waddled round flapping its wings irregularly and out of synchronisation with each other rather like an ill-regulated penguin. Eventually it dug itself a shallow grave in the earth and ground to a halt. Another worked on a 12-volt car battery and called for yards of trailing flex and a hi-tech decoy of extreme complexity, not to mention a set of switches in the hide like the console of an airliner. This apparatus called for a Hercules to carry it and in wet, muddy conditions it taxed the most patient to set it up. You had to dig a considerable hole in the field beneath the decoy in order to conceal the complicated works.

A third involved the decoyer throwing a weighted line over the limb of a tree near his hide, and it calls for little imagination to guess at the tangles which resulted from even that part of the operation. Once the line was stretched taut at a sharp angle from tree to ground, the decoyer hauled up a full-bodied decoy as you would a flag on a halyard. Then at the critical moment he would haul, or allow it to glide down on the principle of a bo'sun's chair. In skilled hands this could be made to look like a pigeon swooping down to land.

Another was made of thin polythene supported by a light plastic framework. This flapper was wound up with a little handle and powered by the ubiquitous rubber band: at a key moment it could be launched from the hide when it fluttered off on its deadly mission. In reality it was just as likely to nose-dive to disaster or fly in a tight circle and, just missing the decoyer's head, bury itself in the depths of a bramble patch.

Yet another immensely complicated piece of high technology

worked by remote control and waddled round giving its wings the odd flick now and then. As this model cost some £2,000 to produce it was unlikely ever to prove a best-seller.

Even the old-timers had a trick up their sleeves and they produced commercially the Bendecoy, which came complete in its wooden carrying case. This was hand-carved out of wood and had a pair of hinged wings. It was driven by an electric motor and powered by a wet-cell electric battery which was kept in the hide. To this day it works well enough in an arthritic sort of way and although I imagine that the Bendecoy must, in its time, have given a lot of people a lot of fun, I doubt if the anonymous inventor (Mr Ben?) made his fortune from it.

A book could be written on the subject of wing flappers alone, and of the keen pigeon shooter inventors who produced them.

After all these rather complicated methods had been tried and found wanting, it was the cheapest and most simple solution which in the end worked best: a cord running from the hide to a cradle upon which a dead bird could be rested, and a mechanical arrangement whereby the decoy unfurled its wings and then returned them to rest (this last was the hardest part). Cheap, easily replaceable, powered by rubber bands, quick to set up and take down and easy to carry, this was better than any of the more complicated, mechanical devices.

A number of flappers found their way onto the market, the best in my opinion being Sid Semark's patent which he got WAGBI (as it was then) to produce, calling it the WAGBI/Semark wing flapper. Sid is an old pigeon shooter and personifies the classic case of the decoyer devising his own equipment; that Sid is a highly skilled craftsman in his own right means that his inventions are going to be efficient. His wing flapper had the dead bird in a cradle, holding it firmly in place, its head impaled on a spike at one end like one of Genghis Khan's victims. Using crocodile clips the decoyer fixes the tips of the dead bird's wings to a wire arm, hinged near the front. Pull the cord which pulls the arms and it is obvious that the wings of the decoy will flick up and forward.

Return power is produced by a couple of Post Office elastic bands: always have a couple of spare ones with you. The cord should be brown, braided terylene which will not show up

FLAPPING AND LOFTING

against the background and, just as important, will not stretch when you give your short, sharp tug — neither will it rot. Wind it onto a frame such as is used in sea-fishing hand-lining outfits, or for keeping garden lines. This will stop it becoming tangled. The peg upon which the decoy is mounted should be stoutly made, of a neutral colour, and fitted with a screw-in eye to guide the line. The whole outfit, flapper cradle, line and peg will fit easily into a small, cloth bag and is ready for use in a moment.

The dead bird you use on the cradle should either have had its wings broken near the body with pliers or be a bird taken

Setting up a WAGBI/Semark wing flapper proud of laid wheat; (inset) Polymer wing-flapper — useful on its day

from the freezer and thawed out. In a freshly shot one, rigor mortis will soon render the bird's shoulder joints very stiff, so much so that when you heave on the line, the decoy does not flap but threatens to come, cradle, peg and all, bodily out of the ground. The joint action must be loose and easy.

Many a day has been wonderfully transformed for me by the use of a wing flapper. Once I was on a field of young rape which the birds had been using heavily, but overnight rain had put them off it for they do so hate getting their feet muddy. My decoys were generally ignored but from force of habit there were pigeons flying to and fro across the field, taking a desultory look at the decoys but not coming in to them. Then I bethought me of my flapper and I set it out a cricket-pitch length away from my hide. That did the trick: two or three quick pulls, just a flash of white and movement, and I could see his head turning in curiosity. He banked round and slid in with every confidence to collapse like a pricked balloon at my shot. I ended the day with eighty-three.

A friend of mine owes his record bag to a flapper. He hurried down late one afternoon having seen the pigeons swooping down a hill, topping a tall hawthorn hedge and settling on the field of rape which lay behind it.

The rape was too tall for static decoys, so Ken set up his decoys on the plough on the other side of the hedge. The flapper set on the edge of the pattern caught the birds' attention and he was able to pull them down to a field which normally they would have had no intention of using. Ken shot 197 before his duties as a gamekeeper called him away and, unselfish sportsman that he is, he allowed one of the farm boys to take his place. The lad killed eighteen more to numerous shots, so if that does not count as a 200-plus day, I don't know what does.

My third example of flapper power took place on a field of ripening wheat, the kernels of which were in that soft milky state much beloved by pigeons. I had managed to set up some Shell decoys which wobbled rather precariously on garden canes and had scattered some dead birds in a small patch of flattened crop. Pigeons had been flying round the field, but I knew that my decoys were not catching their attention: decoying on greenstuff often suffers from this problem. It was high summer, so there was too much leaf on the trees for me to use any lofters so what could I do?

Near my hide stood a massive oak gatepost, old, green and mossy. The top was soft and crumbly and I was able to force in the metal leg on the flapper cradle far enough to give it a firm seat. Unscrewing the metal eye from the flapper peg, I fixed it to the gatepost as near the ground as I could manage, for nettles, thorns and clouds of stinging flies did not make it easy.

I retired to my hide and flapped away: the element of my picture which had been missing was now restored and the last, vital piece of the jigsaw which made the difference between a natural picture and one with something not quite right, fell into place. That was all the pigeons needed and the wing flapper provided the draw, so I killed thirty-six pigeons on a day when I would have been pleased with half-a-dozen.

On its day the flapper is deadly but there are some occasions when it has the opposite to the desired effect. Pigeons will see it in action and shy away — when that happens, take it in and forget about it until the next time you go out. Calling mallard is a similar sort of exercise: one day success, the next which appears identical in every other way, a complete and inexplicable failure. Such things are part of the inexplicable magic of many field sports, and if we had all the answers and could score every time we went out, we would quickly tire of it.

Do not place the flapper too far from your hide; the longer the pull, the weaker the line of communication and the more sluggish the action of the device. Set it on the edge or in the middle of the static decoys; facing the wind is ideal, although the Semark/WAGBI operates from the front so it must be facing the hide no matter what the wind direction. Having said that, a hide which puts the wind at the decoyer's back so that pigeons land into it from in front is the favourite.

Another flapper which works well is the Dead Cert, a carefully thought-out, home-made gadget which operates from the rear and not the front. This bird moves in a very realistic way, is more delicately made than the WAGBI/Semark and works perfectly well.

I had a good day with the Dead Cert when I could not build my hide in the right place due to a shortage of cover under the flightline. A home-made hide in a bare, open field is most

difficult to make and to shoot from so I tried to compensate with a good hide at the wrong end of the field and an inordinate number of decoys. The crop was peas three or four inches high and I had two lofters on their pole poking above the top of a hawthorn.

However, the flightline passed tantalisingly across the far end of the field and only a very occasional pigeon saw, much less responded to, my decoys. I put out the Dead Cert, pulling aside a few pea plants to give it a patch of bare earth on which to operate. This time the passing pigeons, although a good quarter of a mile away, caught the flicker of grey and white, then they saw the static decoys, set their wings and swung round in a great curve to come in to my position. Once you have diverted a flightline, the pigeons coming along behind see the bird in front divert and go in to feed, the ones behind follow them and so on.

When using any sort of flapper, do not overwork it. Two or three quick pulls at the critical moment will do the trick and if that fails, leave it alone. No point in flapping to exhaustion, as some do, even when there is no pigeon to be seen. Wind the end of the cord round a stout stick to give yourself something on which to pull, otherwise the line will quickly make your hand sore.

The Dead Cert and the Semark/WAGBI are the best, but there are some useful home-made ones about. I made one using the tip of a steel tank aerial converted first into a fishing rod, later to a wing flapper. I skinned and preserved a whole pigeon with its wings outstretched and fixed it to the tip of the aerial. The thick end I glued into a stout peg which I hammered into the earth so that the aerial with the pigeon mounted on it stood at a shallow angle to the ground. Placed head to wind, every puff of breeze caused the bird to tilt, dip and soar in a lifelike way. It worked very well, but was awkward and delicate to carry and you could not stop it working. Pigeons would catch a glimpse of it and come for a second look, but it continued to waver and wobble and they would take fright and depart. Peter Steele has invented a similar device which is excellent,

The excellent new flapping decoy invented by Peter Steele of Great Bromley

and manufactured by Shooting Developments under the name of the Fife Swooper.

Archie Coats manages the right effect without any gadgetry at all. He keeps a supply of dead pigeons with him in his hide and when he feels like it, or sees birds passing in the distance, he lobs out a dead bird, not too high nor too far, to land somewhere near his decoys. It is the same principle again, an element of movement in a stationary scene and it is surprising how even such a simple trick can bring pigeons trickling in from distant trees.

Thus we end where we started with the search for the philosopher's stone of movement in the pattern. It doesn't matter really what system you use as long as you are happy with it and can operate it with confidence. Provided it serves as an eye-catcher, then it has done its stuff.

Lofters and flappers — more trouble, perhaps, than a simple squad of static decoys, but part of the up-to-date decoyer's stock in trade. He will manage without them, of course, but the element they add to his flexibility and ability to draw pigeon on bad days is so important that he can consider himself ill-equipped without these two important aids.

6 · Hides

Assuming that the reader has taken on board the foregoing, has his gun, clothing, cartridges, decoys, flappers and lofters, there is still more to carry and more to master. He must be able to hide from the birds, for the carefully nurtured illusion of a peacefully feeding flock of pigeons will be shattered if they see the dreaded human being leaning nearby on a gate-post. The trick is to melt into the background by any of the man-made or natural resources available.

The pigeon is, as we will have grasped by now, a sharp-sighted and oft shot-at bird and it owes its continuing existence to the fact that it is annoyingly quick to observe and respond to signs of possible danger. Thus, he who would seek to ambush such crafty birds must, no matter how good his positioning or decoys, take pains to conceal himself in a way which hides him completely but also allows him to peep out at the view and to wield his gun when the action becomes necessary.

The best material for this is that which grows already in the place where you intend to hide, the hedgerow elders, haw-thorns and firs or the cascading tangle of old man's beard. As pigeons often favour the same flightlines and use them for year after year (subject only to variations of the wind and position of the feeding field) the man who shoots regularly on the same farm will use the same hide many times until it becomes a semi-permanent fixture in the hedge.

By judicious bending, breaking and trimming using the secateurs or straight slasher, the hide-maker simply rearranges that which nature has provided until it makes a suitable, roomy and comfortable hiding place. Room must be left for an entrance and this should be at the side or near the rear or it will spoil the effect. Many a hide has been painstakingly and beautifully constructed only for the maker to realise that he has left no way of getting in and out of the thing, so he has to pull half of it down and start again.

The front, leading edge of the hide should be just above the eye level of a man sitting on his shooting seat. He will be spying *through and not over* his hide: nothing is more off-putting to pigeons than a white face like a rising moon bobbing up and down in an otherwise featureless woodside. The camouflaged clothing, shady hat and strict observance of the rule to *keep still* will ensure that you are not seen.

The decoyer should be comfortable, seated near enough to the front edge of the hide to ensure that he is not seen easily from an angle in front, but not so close that he cannot rise and shoot in a single, fluid movement without demolishing half the hide or catching his gun barrels in the fronds. He must allow room at his feet and behind him for his various accoutrements, bag, spare decoys, poles, slasher, cartridges, sandwiches and other equipment. Make a neat cache of this where you will not be tripping over it or treading on it every time you move.

Right **Wrong**

*An ideal hide has a roof
but room to shoot*

Most sensible shooting folk today use a dog and the pigeon decoyer is no exception. Apart from the pleasure of his un-critical company, he is useful for retrieving wounded birds which might go spiralling down in the distance or set off half-walking, half-flapping to become lost in a nettle-clad dyke. Also such shooting is very good training for a dog, both in steadiness to shot and marking distant droppers. Make allowances for him in the hide so that he may sit or lie down without getting in the way or being uncomfortable. Most dogs like to see what is going on, so leave him a little hole at (his) head height, just to keep him interested. Fail to do this and he will poke his head out of the side of the hide and his move-ments, however insignificant, will be off-putting to the birds. A golden retriever or white-faced spaniel against a dark back-ground can be especially troublesome.

The shooting space must be open and clear with good vision to left and right and room to swing the muzzles for crossing shots and also space for the 'driven' bird which flies in, changes its mind, and comes up and on to land in a tree behind the de-coyer's head. A roof of some sort is to be preferred, no matter how close you press your face to the leading edge. Pigeons are likely to come from any direction, stooping in from on high like peregrines, appearing unexpectedly over your shoulder, approaching directly from behind or hovering out of range

Use elder for hide-making

above you before preparing to swoop down. No roof, and a
pigeon can see every detail of your in-hide secrets.

By a roof I do not mean a weatherproofed, thatched edifice,
but just enough to break the outline of the dreaded human
figure from above — a few stray branches or a frond of elder
will do. If you choose a hedgerow site, it is usually easy enough
to provide the right degree of overhang from established
bushes. The real art of natural hide-making is hard-learned but
never forgotten. I have seen the great Major Archie Coats, in
the time it took me to space and set up a dozen dead bird decoys, create a hide from an apparently solid wall of hawthorn

82

and bramble, with what seemed to me a minimum of effort and very little cutting. The hide was for me, and I sat on the five-gallon drum seat provided and found I had a perfect view of the decoys and the killing area but all the vital angles were carefully screened. One does not make a pigeon hide on most working days for half a century without learning a thing or two.

A very important feature of this particular hide, and something which must always be appreciated was that the basic structure of the hedge was undamaged: what cutting there had been was purely superficial. A hedge may be a hide for a pigeon shooter, but to a farmer it is much more: stock fence, windbreak, a feature which beautifies his farm and a nesting site for his pheasants and partridges. If the pigeon man leaves a place so thin due to his chopping that bullocks break through and stray onto the corn, he will not be welcome again. By the same token, never, *never* cut down hardwood saplings and make them part of your hide. Such trees are slow growing, form the lifeblood of the countryside and should on no account be chopped down for such an ephemeral purpose as a pigeon hide. This is another way to ensure that your permission to shoot is withdrawn in a good deal less time than it took you to obtain it.

By all means cut elder which soon regenerates and which makes good, leafy hides, hawthorn, willow, fir-fronds, bracken, ivy and bramble. All these are little more than weeds and make good cover — the elder has the added advantage of keeping away the flies on a summer's day. After shooting, take in any protruding branches and leave them tucked neatly away from the passage of any agricultural machinery in which they might become entangled, so drawing more earthy curses on your head. The same applies to branches dragged out for mini-lofting of HH decoys: these too must be cleared away when you pack up. The thought of a ten-foot, iron-hard hawthorn branch going through the works of a pea-harvester is not one pretty to contemplate.

The natural hide starts with the great advantage of blending easily, for it uses what is there already, simply rearranging existing materials which are part of the scenery. A refinement of this is the bale hide, a little house built out in the open in

which a shooter can lurk. The great advantage of a bale hide is that it may be placed in exactly the right place, bang in the middle of a huge field, useful because wary pigeons will often keep away from hedges where they know from experience that danger waits, and will land in the middle of a field where they know they are safe. Modern fields are often very large, and the prospect of a 100-acre rape field with only one thin hedge in which to hide can be rather daunting to the shooter, but encouraging for the birds which land far out in the middle of it.

A bale hide, or hides, should be set in position after the crop is drilled, but it is a job for a tractor and trailer. Modern straw bales are weighty affairs and to carry one, much less a dozen, up half a field is beyond most people. The farmer will place the bales for you on any crop he considers is likely to be vulnerable to pigeon damage, but it is a great help if he places them where you want them and not where the farm-worker decides on a whim to drop them. Knowing no better, he will tip them off here and there, possibly missing a well-established and prolific flightline by an infuriating 200 yards.

By now you should have good enough relations with your farmer to be able to plant a coloured cane at the site of each hide so that his man knows where to drop the bales. The bales must be made into a hide immediately or the weather will quickly spoil them and make them difficult to handle. Fifteen bales are needed to make a hide like a palace but it is possible to get away with a dozen. Build a little house three tiers high and square, and you should also have a bale to sit on and another to put on top to hide the dreaded human silhouette. Place the bales cut edge downwards for like this they will keep their shape better, will not sag in the middle and the strings (unless polypropylene) will not rot. As with the hedge-bottom hide, it is important to leave a narrow crack in the hide wall through which you can squeeze and through which your dog can peep. The clear-cut leading edge of the hide should be broken up by two twigs and a scrap of netting, or handfuls of leaves plucked from either the crop or the hedge.

If the bales have been left in the wrong place in a field, hard

An impromptu hide made from old man's beard. The dog likes to see what is going on

luck! Moving them, especially after they have been rained on, is a Herculean job, so make the best of it and depend on your decoying skills to draw the birds from the main flightline. Remember to put a bird high on a stick on the hide itself, for pigeons often like to sit on an unoccupied hide in the middle of a field. A bale hide is a semi-permanent fixture made of natural materials, so the birds become used to it and, unless shot from it regularly, do not see it as a threat.

Many of the heavy bags have been shot from bales, including Archie Coats' 550 birds in a short day. They came with such confidence that eventually he was able to remove the front bale and shoot in almost full visibility, but still the birds came on. It was 'one of those days', and those who wish to read of it fully should get hold of a copy of *Pigeon Shooting* by Archie Coats.

The old rule applies as much to bale hides as to those made of netting or branches — sit down when waiting. For one thing it is much more comfortable than standing, but more important, it gives you a wide and low angle of sky to scan. Bales are popular hides because they are trouble free, comfortable, provide all over, solid concealment, and most important, keep the wind at bay!

Other natural hiding places will occur to a resourceful person: the concept of a hide being four poles and five yards of netting is by no means absolute. An overgrown fence

A netting hide would be easier

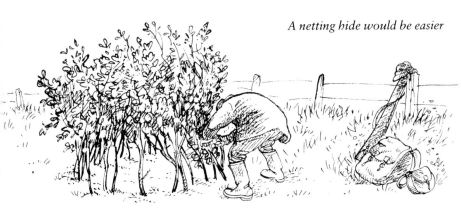

post, a pile of tangled fence wire, an abandoned combine rusting in the nettles and even a mature and savoury-smelling manure heap have each served me well in my time. The manure heap was especially prolific, for pools of brown, stagnant water tend to gather round such mounds. Pigeons grow thirsty, especially in hot weather and when they are feeding on cereals, and they quickly discover such oases and regular flightlines build up. You are unlikely to kill a hundred on such a place, but I have certainly shot up to fifty on a tiny muck-heap puddle — and that more than once! The message is to be adaptable, to 'stay loose', and assess each decoying situation as unique. The whole countryside is one solid mass of places for a human to hide — rather fewer, admittedly, on the sort of fields preferred by feeding pigeons, but they are there to be discerned by the shrewd eye.

I have left until last one of the most often used hiding devices, namely a set of poles and a section of netting, camouflaged to resemble the general hue of the countryside in which it is to be set. This has one great advantage in that the decoyer does not depend on there being a convenient hedge, muck heap or woodside in the key place when he arrives. He carries his hide on his back and can set it up to within a yard of precisely where he wants it. In cold, leafless winter he is not downcast, for he has his own leaves with him. He needn't move any bales, for he can set up a good decoying position in the very key spot in a hundred featureless acres of Hampshire prairie farming.

Basically, the netting hide consists of a patch of green netting and a few sticks on which to hang it. In my early days and long before the custom-made nets and telescopic poles of today, in the true tradition of the pigeon decoyer I made my own. I collected a great number of old nylon stockings and tights (washed ones!) and dyed them green or dark brown, and left some natural. I wove them this way and that through a large piece of cricket stop-netting, hanging the net on the clothes-line while I worked on it. It took an amazing number of stockings to cover the whole area, but I finished it at last. I had a net of generous proportions which would neither rot nor hold water, and was reasonably light to carry. It was rather bulky and the fine nylon tended to catch on briars and pick up every scrap of broken twig, but it was very successful and I used it for many years. It still reposes in its own special kit bag somewhere in the shed.

I have a soft spot for it, but it has been supplanted by other nets which have come along since the makers set about the business of supplying the pigeon shooter. West Dorset Nets make a good one with plastic tags covering a green, rot-proof net; it comes in a dark and a light colour and I recommend the latter every time. Remember clothing and the fact that most outfits were too dark for the background of most pigeon hides? The same applies to hide netting which, for some reason, was also made too dark, chocolate brown and the gloomiest of greens. I imagine that the original Kammo netting used for military purposes was simply adapted, cut into small pieces and sold to keen pigeon men.

However, it is one thing to conceal a tank on a ploughed field or in a plantation of German conifers, but quite another to hide a human being against a background of lime-green, newly sprouted hawthorn. Light-coloured netting is what you need, pale fawn, light green, off-white even and it will blend far more effectively with most hide situations. West Dorset's light version is one of the best of the older types.

Parsons of Nailsea produce a dyed hessian section which is designed to accompany their hide poles. This too works well, is cheap, lightweight and the right colour, though you have to cut a few peep holes in it to avoid the fatal error of looking over the top and giving the game away.

The hide-netting revolution of the last two years has seen the development of Shooting Developments' Leafscreen which solves all the problems in one go. Leafscreen cannot be tangled, a full hide section may be crushed into a little ball for carrying: it is almost impossible to tear, it does not flutter and alarm birds in the faintest breeze and it comes in two colours. The inventor, Allan Graham, tells me that the new, light Grassscreen net is the more popular, but my view is that pigeon shooters have still not woken up to the advantages of this colour.

Countless times I have looked for a pigeon shooting enthusiast I knew to be somewhere in a great field, run my eye along the likely hedge, and instantly spotted the hard, almost black outline of his netting hide. Like an ostrich with its head in the sand, the occupant was perfectly happy: as he had difficulty seeing out of his hide, then it stood to reason that things outside it could not see him. Pigeons, however, would notice this new, dark object and they are no fools, knowing more about what constitutes a bad hide than a good many pigeon shooters. The lives of countless pigeons have been saved by dark clothing, dark netting and the flash of a white face protruding from the gloom.

However, the light, sandy version of Leafscreen, called Grassscreen, is excellent and I have yet to see it bettered. It comes in 12ft 6in x 4ft 6in (3·8 x 1·3m) sections, weighs less than one pound, and compresses into a 15 x 15 x 2in (38 x 38 x 5cm) wad. It is made from fine nylon coated with the appropriate colour of polyurethane. It will stretch to reach an anchoring point, may be cut (but *torn* only with great difficulty) to make spyholes and it is first class in every way. I believe that special sizes may be made to order for anyone requiring a two-man hide, but even then the lightness and compactness are very useful factors.

Cross members in a hide make the difference between comfort and inconvenience. Shooting Developments hide poles have useful clip-on cross members

While on the subject, another brand-new camouflage material has been produced by the same supplier. This is called Spando-Flage which is tubular, stretches almost limitlessly (expansion ratio of 10:1) and can be put to a multitude of uses from scarf, face mask, or barrel stocking to prevent flashes of reflection giving away your position. It incorporates both thermal and ventilation properties and a great length of it will fit into a pocket.

Hide netting forms a part of every decoyer's equipment, sometimes for use on its own, but at its best when used in conjunction with a few broken branches. When set up, the netting may be decorated with clumps of vegetation (leaves or dry grass) taken from the ground in the vicinity of the hide.

The netting will not stand up on its own but must be suspended or stuck up on forked sticks. Seek a place in a hedge or woodside where you can tie a cord from one top corner of the net to quite a high branch on the left and another on the right. The net should not be too high at the corners or it will prevent you spotting pigeons coming from the side, but the cord may be as long as you like. Similarly the foot of the net should be pegged or anchored in windy conditions, for a flapping net is another famous pigeon frightener.

The middle of the net needs a pole, or possibly two. Those cut from the hedge are the cheapest and you shed no tear if you lose one. They do have severe limitations, being heavy to carry and of fixed length: you can cut off a few inches to make one shorter, but no power on earth will make it larger. Three inches either way in a hide can make all the difference between success and failure.

The decoyer will discover, sooner or later, that he needs a set of properly made hide poles. There will be occasions when he can manage without them, but the day will come when their lack will mean that he is unable to shoot from the key position he has chosen. Even a simple thing like a hide pole needs to be right in every respect and these are the features which are important: lightweight, telescopic, robust enough to be jabbed into hard ground, easy to hang a net on, of a discreet colour, and with the facility to fit cross-supports where necessary.

Shooting Developments lofting-cum-hide poles: one of the best

Again, Messrs Parsons make a good set and I believe they were one of the first firms to do so, and their grey-green, aluminium hide poles are still going strong.

The *Shooting Times* pigeon expert John Batley from Gloucestershire has developed a set of hide poles which seem to answer all the requirements and they are marketed by Shooting Developments of Fife. I have already mentioned these poles in connection with the lofted decoy, for the same sections will loft a pigeon and then double as hide poles, thus cutting down on the weight and bulk the shooter needs to carry.

The full title is rather a mouthful, the 'Loft'N'Hide Telescopic Hide/Lofting Pole Set'. A set of four telescopic poles weighs under 3lb (1.3k), about the weight of a box of cartridges, and one pole per set has a kick plate for forcing it into dry or frosty ground — the other poles may be pushed into the

Shooting Developments hide, Leafscreen and guy ropes. Lightweight and effective

holes so made. Each pole extends from 3ft 6in to 6ft 6in (1 to 1·9m) and can be fixed at any desired length by means of a stout wing nut. On good, firm ground on a still day the poles may be driven in and draped with Grassscreen and the hide is self-supporting. In very light soil or on a windy day or if you are using heavy netting, then further support is provided by guy ropes and pegs which come with the set. There is nothing worse than a hide which sags lower and lower during the day and makes it impossible for you to shoot or sit comfortably.

The horizontal supports are an optional extra and may be bought singly or in a set of four. There is a stout nylon clip on each end and these simply fix onto the upright and may be moved up or down to precisely the height required. They also help to make the construction especially rigid. As I explained in the chapter on lofting, three connecting sections of tube allow you to link pole to pole, and at maximum extension you can loft decoys to a height of twenty-five feet (7·6m). Another great advantage of this kit is that it comes complete with its own carrying bag which eases transport and makes it less likely that vital bits will get lost in the grass.

It is a common mistake to believe that every hide must at all times conceal a shooter from head to toe. As with camouflaged clothing, the idea is to break up the outline of the human figure and, provided the occupant obeys the main rule and keeps still, there is no reason why a flimsy hide will not work as well and give better all-round visibility than a more solid construction. Some shooters pile branch upon branch, spread acres of netting and create a virtual fortress which itself may be more conspicuous to the birds than a few carefully arranged pieces of net or elder fronds.

I have an aversion to the man-made hide in an open field, and I do not include bales in this. The Loft'N'Hide set and a large enough section of Leafscreen would probably do the job but with even the best camouflage netting it is very likely that such an object, appearing unexpectedly overnight, would cause birds to shy away. Also, a shooter feels very exposed in such a situation and he must remain absolutely stock-still if he is to have any success. It is hard to make a roof on a hide so placed and the shooter is very vulnerable to passing birds seeing him from above.

A pigeon-shooting friend makes palatial hides, choosing a field such as rape or peas which he knows will be popular with the birds all year and then selecting a key spot beneath a well-established flightline. He drives his Land-Rover to the place, hammers in great stakes with a sledge hammer, nails chicken wire overall, digs a trench with a spade, thatches a roof with straw or reed, and twines more of the same material through the wire. The finished effort would serve as a dugout in World War I and it is certainly a very good permanent hide from which to shoot.

Modern pigeons being less predictable in feeding patterns makes this a hide for the 1960s rather than the 1990s. To go to all that trouble and find that the situation had changed overnight would be heartbreaking. The modern pigeon decoyers must be mobile, with lightweight equipment and be prepared to move, sometimes more than once in the same day. Always take your poles and netting with you, even if you intend to use a bale hide that day, for you might have to move to the far end of the field or even to the field next door. You must remain flexible and adaptable in your approach and set off, full of hope maybe, but with no preconceived notions of how the pigeons are going to behave that day.

Siting, constructing and occupying a hide are specific and important skills which must be mastered. The basic rules are simple enough and like many other things you get better with practice. In time you may, like Archie, be able to put up the perfect hide by any of the methods I have mentioned. When in it you remain still, not bobbing up and down like a yo-yo. You may, if you wish, listen to the Test Match on a portable radio. At least one pigeon-shooting friend makes a habit of it and he tells me it has no adverse effects on the birds whatsoever!

7 · Tactics and Deployment

So there you are, fully equipped with gun, bag, cartridges, poles, nets, decoy, flapper and all the other gear you have either made or bought wisely. However, good equipment on its own does not make a good pigeon shooter, and he must learn how to use it. The modern pigeon is unpredictable, wary and much more difficult to decoy than were its ancestors. He who would outwit it must be able to match it at its own game.

The woodpigeon is a choice and fussy feeder, eating the best, the tenderest and the most expensive. Its gourmet calendar is at its lowest ebb in a cold, hard winter with heavy snow. All that there is left to eat are the brassica, sprouts, kale or cabbages which still poke up above the snow covering. This is poor fare, but beggars cannot be choosers, and the birds feed avidly on this poor stuff which scours them cruelly and actually provides them with little nourishment. The birds lose condition almost overnight and with starvation they lose their natural fear of Man so that they may be knocked down with sticks. To kill a thousand is easy, and you need no gun to do it. Simply keep the birds away from the feeding field for a day and they will not be able to keep alive the flickering spark of life in the night of blistering cold which follows. Their pathetic, half-starved corpses litter the floor of the roosting wood next morning. No one who

94

claims to be a sportsman would take advantage of a fair quarry species when it has come to such a pass and, pest or no pest, they are best left alone.

Following the cold weather, pigeons will be feeding on old stubbles which keep many birds going for weeks. They also feed on the winter-drilled corn, but they do little damage, mainly eating the new-sprouted chickweed which grows among the stalks. When the spring arrives they love the late corn drills, especially those which are badly drilled or in poorly cultivated fields, for then there will be many grains left on the surface. However, the modern high-speed, precision drill makes such places increasingly hard to find, as well as which winter as opposed to spring corn is becoming the norm.

However, spring is still a fat time of year, for the oilseed rape will be starting its new growth of sweet green leaves and pigeons have adapted readily to this modern crop, preferring it to other, apparently more palatable dishes. Rape will keep them going on and off until it is in flower and even then they keep attacking the close-cropped patches, while after it is harvested they love nothing better than its stubble.

They desert the rape in April for fresh hawthorn buds, and will leave everything for a field of peas or beans. Many heavy bags have been shot over this crop when new drilled and handfuls of the seeds are left lying out, easily spotted especially after a shower, tasty and full of nutritional value. Peas can be attacked at any stage, from the day they are drilled to the day before the burned-off stubble is ploughed in. When in doubt, always try the pea fields first.

In a dry season, early sugar beet is often attacked, and it is a general principle that the birds will go for tender greenstuffs when they are thirsty. Young beet is a good crop on which to decoy, being low and sparse so that your decoys shows up proudly. Grass fields are increasingly rare in good pigeon country, and so, sadly, are the clover leys. These were once great pigeon favourites for they loved the coltsfoot, charlock and cockspur which were found there. In hot weather it is also worth remembering that the birds are prodigious drinkers, especially when feeding on grain or dried peas, and a hide by a cattle trough or farm pond will often pay dividends.

The weather will always affect feeding patterns. The birds

hate getting their feet muddy and 'balled' with solid lumps of earth, so when it is wet underfoot they will feed on open fields with bare soil only if they are desperate.

In high summer the fruit trees come into bud and then pigeons can be a real nuisance, taking anything from strawberries (choosing only the best and ripest, of course) to gooseberries, plums and apples. I have taken forty-two apple buds the size of acorns from the crop of a single pigeon. I once shot pigeons on the fruit farms of the Chivers company who make jam. This decoying required me to be in the field at first light on a fine summer's morning, a lovely time of day, full of birdsong and fresh dew; but the pigeons knew well that the early bird catches the worm or, in this case, the strawberry. One by one they came sailing round, preparing to land and walk up the rows, spotting the ripe fruit from the green, taking a peck or two and then moving on. The fruit was ruined and the market price of what the legitimate pickers would have gathered later was decimated. I allowed myself to eat one strawberry for each pigeon I shot, which seemed to me not unreasonable, but I know that the farm foreman did not approve.

In high summer the corn begins to ripen, a hard time for the decoyer what with hordes of stinging flies and most crops too high for his decoys to show. However, it can be a profitable period if you keep an eye on the wheat and barley just before the kernels go hard, when they are still in the soft and pulpy stage. Pigeons love this and make a start by landing on a windblown patch where they concentrate, moving outwards and walking down more of the crop until they have flattened a large area. Birds will often be seen sitting on high tension cables which cross the fields, ready to plunge down and eat some more: this is a sure giveaway that birds are on the 'blown' corn. The decoyer can only hope that the low place is near a hedge or woodside where he can hide and where he can avoid damaging any more of the crop in retrieving his lost birds. A trampling pigeon shooter can do as much damage as any number of pigeons in standing corn.

As autumn approaches, it heralds one of the richest times for all wild creatures. Beech mast, acorns and stubbles (or lightly cultivated ground) are now freely available; many pigeons will be feeding young birds at the nest and working in smaller, scattered flocks. Birds of the year will be recognised by their lack of white collars and comparative gullibility as far as decoys are concerned. With a variety of crops to attack, the pigeon shooter must now be especially vigilant for new feeding patterns, sudden changes of ground and splinter groups of pigeons moving to fresh crops: he must be just as prepared himself to identify and change to a new ground.

As the stubbles are ploughed and Nature's store chest is gradually locked away, feeding once more becomes more concentrated and the flocks begin to build up, sometimes to countless thousands, and they will migrate from Kent to Scotland as the weather and the food supply dictates. The young rape is now sprouting and this is a favourite food source. Rape has been the agrarian revolution of the last two decades, with great acreages suddenly appearing on many lowland farms. There is a possibility that rape growing may be limited by the introduction of a quota system, but it will never be eliminated. Quotas may result in concentrating the birds on fewer fields, rather than the present situation where they have a great choice in every parish, so that at your first shot they leave your field and pour into the one half-a-mile away.

At this time of year ivy berries are often eaten, as are the chippings of sugar beet left behind by the harvester, chunks the size of sugar lumps being eaten easily and found packing the crops of shot birds. Then, gradually, with the onset of the really cold winter weather the birds drift back to the snow-covered greenstuff and our cycle begins again.

It is very important for the decoyer to know the most likely feeding fields at any given time of the year. It will save him many gallons of petrol and wasted hours if his local knowledge and his pigeon intelligence are good enough to take him straight to the half-dozen possible decoying fields.

Once the right field is found and identified, the beginner usually cannot get out of his car quickly enough, and hauls out his decoys, throws them down by a likely bush, makes a hide and waits for the birds to come flooding in. Once per fifty times he just might strike lucky and this will work, but for the other forty-nine he will be disappointed and find himself packing up and moving everything to the far side of the field or even to the field next door. Time spent in reconnaisance (so says

Before and after the erection of Leafscreen

Coats) is seldom wasted and half-an-hour sitting quietly in the car with a pair of binoculars is well spent and might save hours of frustration later.

There is your feeding field with a good flock of pigeons already 'down' and pecking busily. You need to establish the flightline (there may be more than one of them), ie the direction and route the birds are taking to approach your field, for it is under or near this line that you will need to establish your hide. Do not be deceived by one or two birds approaching from a given direction; this may be a fluke or they may be members of

a small, outlying party. Wait until a steady and consistent pattern has emerged and only then decide on the siting of a hide.

A bad hide in the right place is, on balance, better than a good hide in the wrong place, so choose a place right under the main pigeon traffic preferably with the wind at your back — in your face is the least satisfactory. You will have identified the hiding place itself by some natural feature in the hedge, ditch or woodside — ideally it should have the local 'sitty' tree near enough for you to make use of your lofters, but if this tree is under the flightline anyway, it will already be a favourite perching place.

Set your decoys out first, taking the decoy bag about twenty-five good paces out into the field, but further if the birds are wary, closer if the wind is anywhere but at your back. Empty the birds in a heap, and then lob each one in an underarm bowling action to all points of the compass. You have watched feeding pigeon often enough to remember that they feed two here, three there, an odd one somewhere else, but not all equidistant, so lob out the decoys to match that pattern.

Take a look and see that your distribution is good. About twelve dead birds, Shells or HHs will do for a start. Next walk from bird to bird mounting the heads of the dead birds in the manner already described, setting the artificials on their rockers, clearing leaves and twigs which might hinder the movement, and making sure they *generally* face the direction

of the wind. You will have set the decoys on open patches of ground rather than in the growing crops — green ones especially.

Next, set up your hide, working quickly and neatly, chopping, snicking, setting hide poles and draping the net, making sure you have left a doorway, that the net will not flutter and that you have not damaged established timber. Have your gun out of the slip and ready at this time for quite often a silly pigeon will float round for a closer look, quite oblivious of your obvious presence busy with your hide. Leave the gun safely to one side, *unloaded*, but have a cartridge ready in case the easy 'gift' comes in.

Then I spend a few minutes tidying in the hide, trimming brambles, nettles or troublesome twigs which jab you in the

Setting out decoys

Archie Coats takes care in setting up dead birds. No loose feathers and a realistic posture

Place your decoys at irregular intervals, roughly facing the wind

neck, getting your seat comfortable, sorting out the dog and making a cache of your spare equipment. Then give it quarter-of-an-hour before you play the flapper/lofter trump cards.

There is no point in using these devices if the birds are going to come shovelling in of their own accord. Let us assume you are on a field of young rape in early April. Pigeons are flying round and over the field and one or two come to your decoys. Peeping through rather than over the rim of the hide, you watch the bird make its cautious circle and then face the wind for the home run. You have left an attractive gap in your decoys which is to be your killing area. The bird hovers obligingly over this and collapses at your shot. Making sure that no other pigeon was immediately following the first one, you hurry out and set up the dead bird with a piece of wire under its chin.

This killing area is a key feature of setting up a decoy picture.

Pigeon etiquette stops latecomers jumping the feeding queue

Mounting decoys on a branch dragged from the hedge can be a deadly eye-catcher

We know that it is bad pigeon manners to land in front (up-wind) of a feeding flock, so a shrewd decoyer leaves a gap which tempts the bird to land where he wants it to. Needless to say, this gap is situated to give the shooter the best possible chance of an easy shot. This killing area must not be filled with dead birds as they accumulate, but must be left clear. My favourite shape of pattern is the 'comma' which leaves a good killing area behind the main 'blob' of the bunch. A U- or V-shaped picture is also effective: sometimes when using a bale hide, your decoys may be divided into two distinct and separate groups tempting incoming birds to land between them.

On this occasion things are not easy, so we decide to try a lofter, assembling the poles and dropping two full-bodied decoys into convenient forked twigs twenty feet up the 'sitty' tree. This ruse makes the pigeons more confident and they come to land in the tree and you begin to build up a reasonable score. As the tally mounts, you take in your artificials and replace them with dead birds, waiting for a lull before leaving the hide — unless, that is, you have a dead bird lying on its back or a big patch of feathers which will make the pigeons shy away.

Then a huge flock, three hundred strong, comes as if to settle about your very ears. Some say leave such a flock alone or move it gently on without firing a shot and frightening it too much. It is a point of view, but my opinion is that a bird in the hand is worth two in the bush and I should have a try at them.

Then you notice to your annoyance that a few pigeons have settled in on the far end of your field and your static decoys, even when enhanced by a wing flapper, are giving away too much weight when it comes to a competition with real pigeons. Even as you watch, more pigeons go spiralling down to the rival 'picture' and the flock grows rapidly. So then you fire a shot, a waste of a 10p cartridge perhaps, but it moves the flock and scatters it and you are in with a chance again. If fresh birds persist in landing far from your hide, you must improvise a scarecrow. A strip of white polythene tied on to a bendy stick and jabbed into the ground in the offending places will keep the pigeons off for the rest of the day, and then they will respond to the less disturbed scene which you have prepared for them.

Two 'killing areas' temptingly placed in the decoy pattern

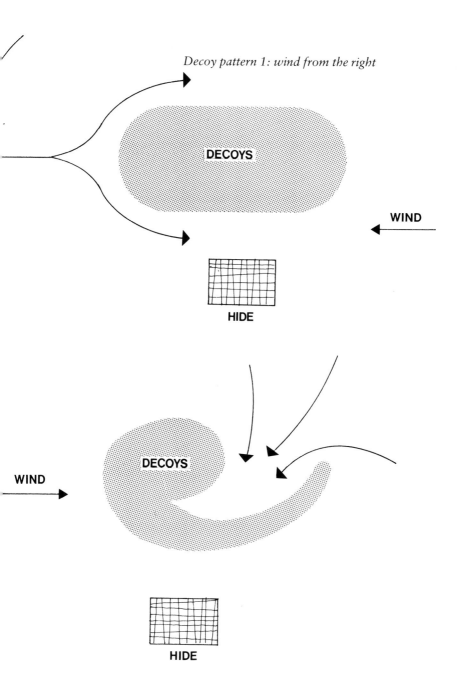

Decoy pattern 1: wind from the right

DECOYS

WIND

HIDE

WIND

DECOYS

HIDE

Decoy pattern 2: wind from the left

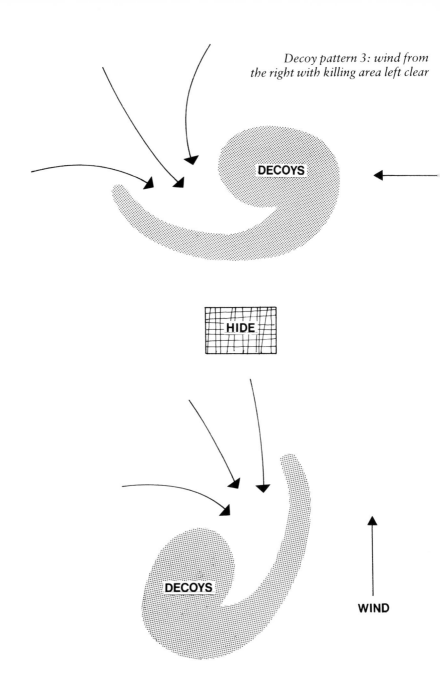

Decoy pattern 3: wind from the right with killing area left clear

Decoy pattern 4: wind from behind with killing area left clear

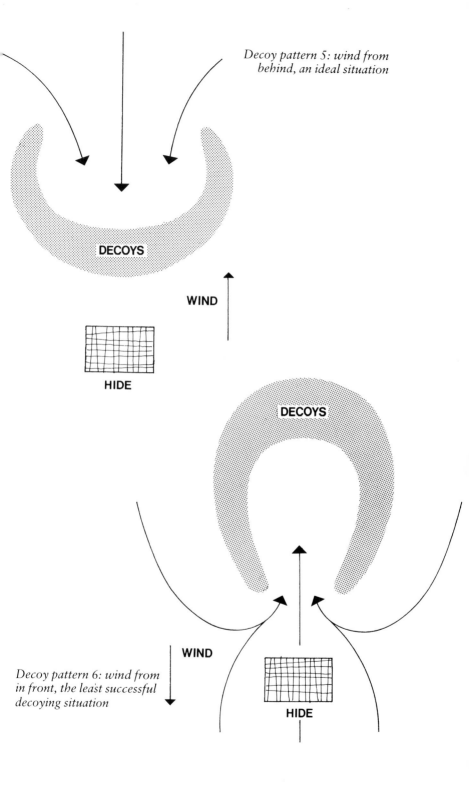

Decoy pattern 5: wind from behind, an ideal situation

DECOYS

WIND

HIDE

DECOYS

WIND

Decoy pattern 6: wind from in front, the least successful decoying situation

HIDE

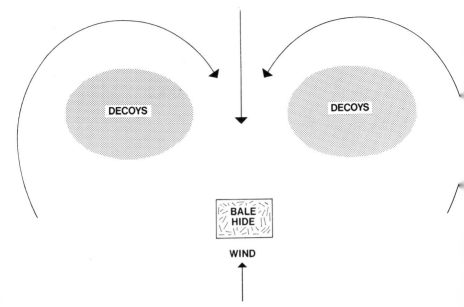

Decoy pattern 7: two squads of decoys, wind from behind

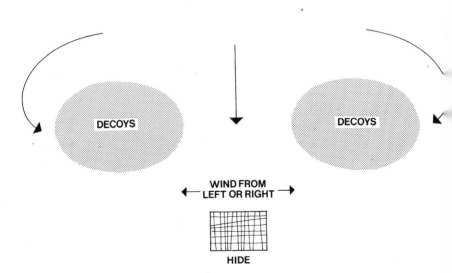

Decoy pattern 8: two squads of decoys — equally effective for a side wind from either direction

Quite often, and more so these days, pigeons will use the field next door to the feeding ground as a resting/digesting area. This may be turned to your advantage, especially if the feeding crop is tall and it is difficult to display your decoys. The resting field is usually plough, cultivated land or newly sprouting corn on which it is easy to show decoys to advantage. You may decide to move your stall onto this field in preference to the feeding field, putting a few low lofters on the hedge at the same time.

On a corn, bean- or pea-drill you will have to judge whether or not the popularity of the field with the birds is likely to be maintained. There may have been a thousand on it the day before yesterday but large seeds like peas and beans are conspicuous, easily seen and eaten, and a thousand pigeons can manage a surprising amount between them in a day. Not only will observation of pigeon movements help your decision, but a close look at the surface of the field will show you if any seeds remain lying around. If there are none and few signs of pigeon in the area, you are too late for they have cleared it, and there is little point in setting up there.

Let us say that some time during our mythical day on the oilseed rape, the pigeons suddenly stop coming — an event which these days is all too common. If it is late in the afternoon you might as well pack up and go home for they will be unlikely to return that day. Should it happen to be mid-morning, you have two choices: the birds have either gone to a wood or a resting field to digest or, due to your presence, they have shifted their ground.

It is hard to guess which it is, but if there is passing pigeon traffic, it is possible the birds are feeding elsewhere. In this case, the mobility and ease of unpacking and packing your equipment will prove especially useful. Watch the next pigeon to pass over and follow it with your eye or with your binoculars until it vanishes over the horizon. It was sure to be going somewhere. Go to as near the place it vanished as you can drive and wait for the next pigeon which ought to come on the same line. You should not have to repeat this process too many times before you find the new feeding ground. This is a desperate measure but I have used it several times to good effect, although it has been known to go wrong.

Keep below the hide, rise smoothly and shoot in one movement

When in the hide it is important to maintain strict discipline. Keep still and scan the skies from your *seated* position. Do not react when pigeons approach but look up from under your hat brim, moving your head as little as possible. When the bird is fully committed and at the last moment, rise and shoot in one smooth movement. If you are a percentage shooter you will take only easy birds which have come in to the killing area and hovered suicidally or wafted gently past. Take these and these only and you will be able to boast of your ratio of kills per cartridge. If you take your pleasures less seriously you will have a go at every bird within killing range, even those passing well

over with no intention of landing among your decoys. However, unless you are an exceptional shot, your percentage of kills will not be remarkable, for a quick, alert and alarmed pigeon takes some hitting.

Keep an eye on the dog — he will be happy if you have provided him with that little peep-hole, but do not let him run in to falling birds. However, should a wounded bird fall and begin to walk away from the decoys, send the dog immediately or fetch it yourself, for such a bird is a very strong draw to others.

Close observation and a positive effort to follow the Coats maxim and 'think like a pigeon' will help you in your decoy deployment. Watch closely how birds approach your pattern and how they react. Pigeons like to fly along the edge of a feeding

113

bunch looking for a place to drop in. If your decoys are placed, say, thirty yards out and the incoming pigeons fly along the far edge, they will be out of range. They may not fly along the near edge because it is too near the hedge and thus a danger. A shrewd decoyer would react to this by moving his decoys not nearer but *further* away, thus attracting pigeons to the near side. I have seen this dodge used more than once to good effect. Generally speaking though, it is wise to set your decoys further from the hide than was once accepted practice. If you can draw a wary pigeon well enough for it to circle low, that might be the best chance that you could expect on a hard day. The easy ones which hover over the killing area are greatly to be desired, but they too are not as regular as of yore.

If pigeons come and then shy away at the last minute, something is wrong. Your hide is inadequate, the decoys shine, there is a dead bird lying on its back, too many scattered feathers or any of many possibilities. Do not leave things and hope for the best, but examine your pattern, move some decoys, take in any artificials which seem to be catching the light (most common in rain or bright sunlight), tidy up the feathers and try different layouts. Trial and error and, eventually, experience will improve the situation.

When arriving at your field and finding it covered with birds, you must not creep up and shoot 'into the grey' for this alarms the whole flock in one go and when they depart they may never return. Walk them off, for all the world a farm-worker or hiker going about his lawful business and the birds will not be unduly frightened and are more likely to come trickling back after you have set up.

In short, use your imagination and your knowledge of pigeons to help you. Do not act in the same old stereotyped way every time: watch the field, see what the birds are doing and where they are settling and try to reproduce that with your decoys as closely as possible. Use little clods or hillocks to show decoys to advantage, be ready to move if you have got it wrong or the birds change their ground, and generally *stay loose!*

Let us hope that our decoyer has had a good day and killed forty pigeons. He must now pack up. This job must be done logically and carefully so that his gear is all ready for next time.

Throw the dead pigeons into a heap, taking care to save the wire head supports. Stack the Shells and take care to keep the pegs which are easily lost. Dead birds go in a sack, decoys in the carrying bag.

Then dismantle the hide, rolling the netting carefully, taking down the poles, wiping off mud, and packing everything away. Restore the hedge as best you can, replace the dead branches you have dragged out if you want no curses from the farmer. Pick up all used cartridge cases and have a final check to make sure your knife, secateurs or other valuables have not been left lying in the grass. A wise man puts these in bag or pocket immediately after use, but some of us are not wise men.

When all that is done you plod slowly off towards your transport, conscious of a good day's sport, of fieldcraft applied, of a wily adversary outwitted and of the farmer's crop protected. There are many worse feelings!

8 · Farmers and Permission

Finding pigeon shooting is not especially difficult but it is far less easy than it was twenty years ago. The huge flocks certainly do a great amount of agricultural damage in a year at a national cost of many millions of pounds. Some crops recover from pigeon damage but some do not and many farmers would shed no tear if the last bird were to fall and the race became extinct.

The scene is not a free-for-all. Some farmers have regular shooters who cover their ground so there is no room for a stranger. Others may have had bad experiences of 'pigeon shooters' disturbing stock, poaching game, damaging good trees, lighting fires and trampling down the crops. Even the pigeons are preferable to that! Other places may be high-powered pheasant shoots where the keeper does not wish to have his birds disturbed at critical times of the year by indiscriminate shooting. Another farm may be in the hands of a shooting syndicate which wishes to keep the pigeon shooting for itself. Still another may have cashed in on current interest in the sport and let its pigeon shooting through the columns of

Shooting Times magazine.

There is nothing for it but to knock on doors. Find the feeding flock and go and ask permission, not from a farmer busy with milking or struggling to extricate a load of potatoes from a muddy gateway, but when he is likely to be in a pleasant frame of mind. Steel yourself for a negative response and if you are given one, raise your hat politely and retire gracefully. If you go in dirty overalls, unshaven, and in hob-nailed boots you might receive a dustier answer than if you had gone clean and tidy. Be polite; you are asking for a favour, not bestowing one.

You may end up dealing with a keeper where the same principle applies, and if he is kind and helpful, you should let your appreciation be known in a tangible manner.

Once you have been given permission, treat your good reputation as your most valuable possession. It takes half a minute for your privileges to be withdrawn, privileges it might have taken you some months to win. Remember at all times that you are a guest on the farm and take no advantage of this hospital-

Don't ask a farmer for pigeon shooting, when he is obviously busy . . .

ity. It is very hard to get away with anything for long in the countryside and the locals have an uncanny knack of knowing what is going on. If you abuse your position and shoot a pheasant (for you may have many chances to do so), allow your dog to pester sheep, leave open a vital gate or flatten half an acre of standing corn with your antics, a word will quickly be dropped into the right ear and then suddenly there is one less farm on your books.

If you have the sense you were born with, it stands to reason that you will go out of your way to show them what a good chap you are. Make friends with farm-workers and always stop for a quick word; a bottle at Christmas, keeping the farmer informed of your comings and goings and not disturbing his Sunday rest by shooting near his house, are all common courtesies and a part (I should have thought an obvious part) of the common sporting code.

If you are seen to be doing a good job, keeping off the pigeons and not blotting your copybook, you will become a welcome friend on the farm. Your farmer will tell the farmer next door what a paragon you are and your shooting ground will increase. Bring a friend, but ask permission first. In time, who knows, you may be asked to join the end-of-season cock shoot or even to take on the game shooting yourself on a small farm where this is not organised already.

. . . naturally all livestock must be respected

This happy state will give you the freedom to operate over a wide area as the feeding flocks move from place to place. It might be unreasonable for you to expect exclusive rights, and it is possible that there will be other keen pigeon shooters covering the same ground. You will learn to give and take: first come first served is the rule, and it is not 'done' to set up on a field which is already occupied, unless the field is a large one. If this is the only place available, have a word with the earlier arrival and make sure that you will not be in his way: expect him to do as much when your roles are reversed.

You may find that your farmer hedges his bets and covers his vulnerable fields with a battery of bird-frighteners. Today these may take many weird and wonderful forms, and are a far cry from the straw-stuffed Wurzel Gummidge 'mawks' of yesteryear. Overhead fly red balloons, and kites in the shape of eagles; carbide guns shatter the peace of the countryside with drum-splitting bangs. Far worse, and which epitomise noise pollution, are the high-pitched sirens attached to bangers — they are so loud that they can cause ear damage if you are careless, and when not turned off at night (as they should be) they keep whole village populations awake.

Pigeons quickly grow accustomed to most of these devices and will feed very close to a gas gun, barely lifting from the ground when it goes off. On arrival at a field, a decoyer should

A sight to catch the eye of a decoy shooter — and also a farmer!

turn off these guns by means of a simple tap on the cylinder, but he should also remember to turn them on again when he leaves. Some farmers believe that pigeons have learned that these sudden bangs mean a good feeding field and that, instead of driving them off, they actually attract them. There is now a strong lobby which seeks to have banned some of the more anti-social types of bird-scarer and who knows, by the time this book is published, restraints may have been imposed. . .

Finding and keeping good ground are major preoccupations of any shooting man, the pigeon decoyer no less than the rough-shooting pheasant man or wildfowler. If you find that it is difficult to break into the local circuit, one option is to join the local pigeon and/or rabbit clearance society. The BASC-sponsored groups sprang up about ten years ago when like-minded individuals joined ranks and, in return for offering farmers crop protection, found shooting for themselves. Most districts now boast such a club and members are given prompt access to good pigeon ground where, on their own, they might have spent years finding a foothold. Usually a period of apprenticeship is required and also actual proof that the new member is to be trusted on cherished club shooting.

In addition to the pigeon shooting, the recruit to a club will quickly make new shooting friends, for the lone shooter can feel rather isolated living in a street occupied by the hostile or the indifferent. Most clubs also have film evenings, visiting speakers and educational sessions so that by joining, a whole new world will be opened.

I return to my original theme, namely that it is by knocking on doors and being prepared to weather the frequent rejections that a would-be pigeon shooter can find himself a corner in which to set up his stall. Difficult? Maybe, but ask any pigeon man how he started and he will tell you the very same. Once you have found somewhere the worst is over, and thereafter things become progressively easier. 'I shoot on Farmer Green's place and he thinks I am doing a good job,' you say — a sound introductory remark. You know that the moment you have driven away, the new man will be on the phone to Farmer Green, and it is during that critical conversation that your whole reputation and your previous performance are on the line. The Green/new man conversation will determine much of your future as a shooting man in that parish. If all is well, like a line of dominoes, the available farms will fall before you.

Make a friend of the farmer: between you, you ought to enjoy a good relationship. He wants the pigeons shot, you want the sport and the result, if you have played your cards right, ought to be two satisfied parties.

Although often the highlight of the day, lunch should be a simple affair

9 · Roost and Flight Shooting

When the decoys lose their attraction in the bitter and hard month of 'February Filldyke' ('February Frostbound' is a more likely name for it if recent changes of weather patterns are anything by which to judge), the decoyer casts his eyes to the roosting wood. In the winter months the birds flock in to these sanctuaries from mid-afternoon to sundown, although during the game-shooting season, keepers and syndicate pheasant shooters are not happy about pigeon men blasting away in the woods just when their precious pheasants are drawing in and preparing to go up to roost. A month or so later, the game birds are thinking about nesting so disturbance at the end of March is equally unwelcome.

Nice to be able to stroll out on a pigeon-shooting foray unbowed by the usual massive burden of decoys, net and poles under which you are accustomed to staggering. All you need is the gun and a bag of cartridges and, if you are wise, your trusty gundog. If your instincts are affronted by not having to carry

Ignore the twigs when you shoot

half a hundredweight, you can always take a set of lofting poles and a couple of full-bodied decoys with you.

Thinking like a pigeon (of course) you will appreciate that a bird dropping in to the roosting wood would, with reason, expect to see a few earlier arrivals already occupying the favourite twigs. Thus it might be no bad thing for the roost shooter to 'salt' the woodside trees with some sitting birds to give later arrivals a sense of confidence. Just think that, as a pigeon, you would probably land in a roosting tree far more directly and confidently if you saw a few pigeons there already than you would if you encountered only naked twigs.

Someone used to handling lofting poles will have no trouble putting a couple up a tall, bare tree near a clearing and this will often make a deal of difference. The pole with a double bracket may be left in position.

Roost shooting will tend to produce harder, more challenging shots than decoying. Usually the birds will be swift-flying crossers or overhead shots and they take some hitting, especially through a frieze of twigs. A windy night is by far the best, for a gale causes the birds to drop in as soon as they can to the shelter of the roosting wood. On a calm night they will circle endlessly at great height and seem to be able to see every inch of you, no matter how carefully you hide. On a still night the sound of your shots seems very loud, reverberating round the trunks and seeming to carry a great distance, thus disturbing pigeons on their way in — on a windy night the bangs are carried away.

When you get to know your favourite wood well, you will realise that some parts of it are more favoured than others by roosting pigeons. Ivy-clad trees are favourites for they provide warm shelter, and birds often prefer to use the side of the wood away from the prevailing wind. Another important factor in your choice of hide position is having room to shoot. If you can wait by a little clearing, so much the better, and you need not be put off by a thin tracery of twigs high above your head; however, if the twigs are bushy and low they will knock great holes out of your shot pattern. In the same way, thick boughs are to be avoided for it seems always to happen that just as you

Find an open place from which to shoot

Be careful not to get snagged up in hedgerows

are about to pull the trigger at an easy bird, you cover a great branch and shoot straight into it.

There is no need to make a large and complicated hide. Stand by an ivy-clad trunk or low bush making sure that you have a good field of vision and keep absolutely still. You should wear green and brown clothing, mittens and a floppy brimmed hat — these last two items are especially important for just remember how conspicuous is the full moon of a human face bobbing about in the undergrowth. For this reason, some roost shooters go to the length of wearing a face mask, which may take the form of a green veil hanging from the hat brim or a length of Spandoflage worn as a balaclava helmet. I have never felt at ease when wearing face masks for

No proper hide is necessary for roost shooting

they are scratchy, hot and claustrophobic, but many shooters use them regularly. An alternative is a green stick of camouflage make-up as worn by marine commandos on active service. That seems to me a little extreme. Keep still and move your eyes rather than your whole head and look up from under your hat brim and the birds will not see you.

Roost shooting is a simple enough technique provided you are a reasonable shot, but many roost shooters suffer from the same complaint, a contagious one called lack of patience. They simply cannot resist having a hopeful shot at great passing flocks which are miles out of range, and do it because they hear distant shots from other woods, imagine that other shooters are enjoying grand sport and begin to feel left out of it. Thus they have a hopeful stab at the next pigeon to pass high overhead. The real beneficiaries of this foolishness are the cartridge manufacturers, for the amount of ammunition wasted on organised roost shoots is enough to start a war.

The other result of this over-eager shooting is that the pigeons are disturbed and quite naturally go on to investigate another wood where no danger is waiting. The answer is simple self-restraint: imagine that each cartridge costs £1 and that your kills per cartridge performance will be published for all to see in next week's copy of *Shooting Times*. High, circling pigeons are only having a look-see to make sure that the coast is clear before coming round on a second and third circuit, lower each time prior to making the home run. The roost shooter should be patient during these early manoeuvres and pick his moment when the birds are at their easiest.

When a chance presents itself, wait until the last moment before moving, for the bird will spot you very quickly and twist and jink to safety. Rise smoothly, swing, allow plenty of lead and fire one careful shot. Forget about the second barrel: too many roost shooters cannot wait to loose off their postman's knock of a double shot. Keep it as an emergency for a second chance. As usual, pick your bird if a flock comes and on no account ever blaze away into the thick, for you will certainly miss.

If a grand army arrives, pick a straggler or outlier and take your chance, but do what you can to avoid startling the main lot and preventing their return. Forget the twigs, and shoot as

A roost shooter must be quick to shoot in an enclosed place

though you were in open country. If you try timing your shot to coincide with a thin place or a little gap, you will end up 'poking' and missing miserably. By swinging properly you may have the occasional shot spoiled by branches but you hit more that way than trying to snap shoot through little gaps.

The roost shooter will have his back to the wind as birds will land into it, so most of his shooting will come from the front. However, he must have eyes in the back of his head and a well-developed sense of peripheral vision, for pigeons will sneak in very quietly and very low from any point of the compass and he must be ready for them.

Halfway through the afternoon on a February day is about the time to arrive. This gives you time to study the wood, find the places where droppings have accumulated showing the favourite roosting trees and to choose a suitable hiding place. Birds will begin to arrive quite early, numbers building up as time passes. No point in waiting until last light, for you will disturb roosting pheasants, and there comes a moment which you will come to recognise, when the flow simply dries up and no more birds will arrive.

If you feel the occasion merits it, you can set a squad of static decoys on the field by the edge of the wood. Pigeons tend, as a rule, not to feed so close to woods, but they are also greedy birds and often cannot resist a last few beakfuls before bed-time. Decoys on the downwind side might draw incoming pigeons to land among them or bring them in low to land in the woodside trees, both situations on which the shooter can capitalise. Take in your decoys before it grows too dark, as fumbling about in the gloom searching for your last Shell rocking peg can be a testing experience. Nonetheless, there are days when this decoying dodge works very well.

February is the traditional time for the organised roost shoot, the brainchild of the NFU and seen by them as an opportunity to destroy great numbers of crop despoilers in one go. The lone roost shooter is liable to drive the pigeons to a wood three fields away and once pigeons have started to go down in a place away from the one he wants them to use, they tend to draw all the later arrivals. The organised roost shoot theory is that every wood, copse, clump, plantation and spinney in the parish is manned on the same afternoon. The grapevine and the sporting press usually establish when this will be, but it often falls on the first or second Saturday in February.

The pigeons are driven from one wood by a volley of premature shots and set their sights on the next place down the road, but there an equally hot reception awaits them. Thus they go everywhere and are driven from pillar to post seeking a quiet place, growing more tired and keener to roost as the evening draws on. They have to land some time and the theory is that large numbers are shot in this way. The trouble is that due to Sod's Law the second Saturday in February is a day of flat calm and a touch of spring in the air, so the pigeons fly round quite happily, miles out of range, and come in in a rush at last light. Also every farm lad armed with a rusty fowling piece is not necessarily a good shot and, Sod's Law again, it is towards those gunners that the birds inevitably fly.

However, we all dutifully turn out on Pot-a-Pigeon day, knowing full well that we may not get many decent chances and that the NFU might be disappointed with the results. In fact, the way to destroy a great number of pigeons is to keep them from their feeding ground in snowy, bitter cold weather. If you are protecting the only field of sprouts in the parish and if that is the only feeding above the snow available to the birds, they will be unable to charge their batteries sufficiently to see them safely through the cold night to follow. Rake-thin and starved they will drop dead off the branches in the roosting wood. This book is not concerned with such practices for they are unsporting and the woodpigeon, pest or no pest, deserves better treatment at our hands.

Far better and allied to roost shooting is flighting, and many consider this the cream of the sport. Good local knowledge is essential here, for this sport depends on the shooter knowing the main flightlines for this area. When pigeons have finished feeding for the day they set off, not only in great flocks but in long strings to head for the roosting wood. They use local landmarks on the way — a high tree or a line of trees, a huge solitary hawthorn, the corner of the farm buildings — and fly over them every night. In the Fens these flightlines are especially conspicuous for landmarks are few and far between so the pigeons' favourites soon become well known.

Our birds trickle up from many feeding fields far out in the flat Fens and gradually begin to funnel in along the stark lines of poplars and the straggly hedges, making always for the higher ground and the great woods in the parks where they intend to pass the night. The flightline becomes thicker the closer it gets to the wood, so that at the right time in the right place, there is a regular succession of passing pigeons. As in most forms of pigeon shooting, a stiff headwind is a most useful asset. Usually the birds fly well out of gunshot of the ground: having been shot at regularly has taught them the wisdom of that. But when there is a gale in their beaks they must battle into it, losing height and side-slipping to seek out a line of less resistance, but determined not to give up.

This the flight shooter's golden opportunity, for he seeks out a favourite pigeon landmark and hides as close to it as he can and simply takes his chances as the birds struggle over. He may

In heavy snows, Brassicas are all that the pigeon has on which to feed

need to move his position to left or right if the wind comes at a slight angle to the flightline, for while the birds might aim for a landmark they may have to settle for passing it some distance to left or right as the wind dictates. Just watch the early birds and be prepared to change your position at short notice. Hedges or ditches make ideal places for this shooting and you need no decoys nor your usual load of equipment. Camouflaged clothes, floppy hat, gun and bag of cartridges should do the trick.

In spring this year a mighty hurricane swept over the Fens, tearing out great trees, hurling tiles from village roofs and making even the simple act of standing up in the open difficult. The gale was from the south and our parish pigeons flight in from the north so just for once, the combination was perfect. My young son was straight down the Fen after school and he had a splendid evening's sport with his twenty-bore. He hid in a reedy dyke and was able to nip smartly to left or right in time

to intercept each approaching party of birds as he spotted them in the distance.

He did well for a young lad, but two rather more experienced old hands on the farm next door shot no less than sixty-one in the short dusk, which only goes to show what can be done in the right conditions and in the right place. Even in winds far less severe than that one, pigeons will fly in far lower than they would like and the flight shooter needs only to keep an eye on the church weathercock and note the strength of the wind and his local knowledge will do the rest.

Sometimes a form of flight shooting is possible during the day as birds move from one field to another. A fair amount of luck attends the operation, for the birds must be using both fields in rotation without any particular preference for either, so that they are flitting from one to another during the day. The fields should be far enough apart so that your shooting does not disturb them. By recognising what is going on, observing the flight lines and knowing your ground, you ought to be able to place yourself on a point suitable to intercept the birds and, if you have got it right, they will approach you from two opposite directions. Sometimes a sudden shower of rain will make the birds desert a muddy field in favour of a clean one for, as we have established, they hate getting their feet muddy and 'balled'.

Similarly you may intercept a flight line at the feeding end rather than the roosting end but again, you must not be so close to the feeding field as to risk disturbing all the birds in one go. Good sport may be had as the birds begin to trickle off on their way home to roost or even for a midday rest in the trees. They tend to be relatively unsuspecting at such times and a short, sharp shoot may result from your little piece of field strategy.

In these unpredictable days for pigeon shooting, it is often possible to shoot as many birds by careful flight shooting as by field decoying, but you need to be observant, adaptable and aware of changing pigeon behaviour to do so.

Birds shot flighting, or roost shooting can be amongst the most sporting targets possible. This is no poor man's sport, but shooting to test the best and many a star of the covertside has been made to look quite foolish by an apparently easy overhead pigeon. They fly more quickly than it seems, react with amazing speed at the hint of a movement below or flash of an upturned face, and jink three yards across the sky at the blink of an eye as the shot streaks past. Upwind or downwind, a woodpigeon takes some hitting, and roost shooting or flighting can show it at its best.

*Some dogs do not care
for the pigeon's loose
feathers*

10 · Stray Feathers

Dogs Pigeon shooters tend to be divided sharply down the middle on the matter of dogs. Some say that a dog is a liability: it gets in the way in a crowded hide, its movements can give away your position and it might cause trouble with nesting game or farm animals. All these are reasonable points, but assuming that your dog is fairly steady, I would prefer to take him along. For one thing, a pigeon hide can be a lonely place especially on a 'cold' day, and, as any wildfowler will confirm, your dog can be a good companion.

From the practical point of view it is often useful to be able to pick up a 'walking wounded' pigeon quickly and cleanly before it draws away incoming birds, and without the trouble of struggling in and out of your hide. It is also very good training for a dog, which will pay dividends later on when you are game shooting. The dog learns not to run in, to mark distant droppers and in time learns to distinguish between the freshly killed bird which you want retrieving and the decoy which you do not.

The dog should not be given too many retrieves in a day and then only at carefully selected subjects. Even an old dog will tire of retrieving pigeons, for the loose, powdery feathers fill his mouth and he cares for this not at all. Young dogs can be put off retrieving for ever by carrying freshly shot pigeons too often, so be careful not to overdo it.

Droppers which fall dead or dying from a branch on the far side of the field may be hunted out, provided it is not the game nesting season, and a dog is ten times as good at this as a flat-footed human. All these experiences will serve to keep a dog sharp and keen in the out-of-season months when, but for pigeon shooting, he would spend most of his time asleep in the kennel.

Obviously your dog won't run in . . .

I always take a dog pigeon shooting

Wounded birds It is a sad fact of shooting that now and then a wounded bird will come to hand: would that it were not so, but we have to face the fact. A pigeon shooter must, as well as any other live quarry shooter, make himself an expert at dispatching wounded birds. The job must be done quickly, humanely and at the very earliest opportunity.

The amateur does one of two things, either twirling the bird round by its head or pulling the head with a heave strong enough to decapitate a lion. Pigeon heads seem to be rather loosely attached, and both these methods tend to produce the same result, head in one hand, bird in the other, and a bloody mess in between. This is a miserable performance which leaves you with a spoiled bird, a feeling of inadequacy and the sense of a job badly done.

Experts hold a bird by the head, give it a sharp, downward jerk and dislocate the neck without decapitation. This is a knack, acquired after practice and well worth mastering.

An alternative is to hold the bird round the body and give its head a sharp tap against a solid object such as a fence post or branch but *never*, as is sometimes the case, the stock of your gun.

Certain, clean, quick and safe are the patent pliers supplied by Shooting Developments or by Sid Semark, which clamp onto the neck of any wounded gamebird from a snipe to a goose and one quick squeeze crushes the spinal column and kills the bird instantly. This is foolproof and the pliers are small and light enough to be carried on all field shooting occasions.

Lastly is the old fashioned 'priest', so called because it was used to administer the last rights to fish. It is a short, weighted, miniature club made from a length of stag-horn or stick and it works well for birds also. Simply hold the bird in one hand and give it a sharp crack where the head meets the neck: crude, but effective.

The whole matter may not be to everyone's taste, but the responsible shooter has a moral duty to get it right. At least be grateful that I do not advocate the old keeper's method which involved biting into the cranium of the bird using the canine teeth to crack the skull. Effective, but ughhh!

Dead pigeons Treat the quarry with respect when you have bagged it. Pigeons abandoned in heaps in polythene sacks or piled in a car boot will not last long. It is a crime to spoil good meat thus, and your worthy adversary deserves better treatment. At the end of the day remove the crop from each bird, simply pulling and tearing away the tightly packed ball. This will not damage the meat in any way and will keep the bird in a better state of preservation than if it were left. The damp vegetable matter, especially if it is greenstuff, will quickly ferment and spoil the bird. The job takes only a few seconds per bird and is well worth it.

Carry the birds in a hessian sack, an object harder to find nowadays than once upon a time. On no account use polythene, for this useful material causes meat to go 'off' more quickly than anything. A good old-fashioned sack allows the air to circulate.

When you get them home, lay the birds in rows on their backs on a concrete floor out of the sunlight. Here they will cool naturally, and not sweat; they go stiff and firm and remain in good condition for the game dealer or for use as decoys next time you go out. Like dispatching wounded game, care of the bag is the moral responsibility of every sportsman.

Some shooters buy an old ice-cream freezer and keep it in the garage for storing pigeons until they have sufficient to make a game-dealer visit worthwhile. This is a sound idea, but you must expect a lower price from the game dealer for frozen birds than for fresh ones. I always like to produce birds of which I can feel proud rather than ashamed — to me this is an integral part of the sporting ethic.

Safety The fact that the pigeon shooter usually operates alone does not lessen the importance of safety with the gun. A man alone is apt to grow careless and complacent, leaning a loaded gun against a twig while he nips out to adjust his decoys. One slip, stagger or careless dog could mean a ghastly accident. He takes such dangerous short-cuts in case a pigeon may suddenly come and catch him unawares, but the time it takes to slip in a cartridge is nothing to set against such a risk.

Pigeon men have met accidents in some almost unbelievable ways. Loaded guns have been dragged, barrels first, through hedges. Loaded guns have been carried over wobbly barbed wire fences by men heavily burdened by half-a-hundredweight of pigeon shooting gear. Loaded guns have been leaned against a flimsy filigree of hide netting, the stock leaning against the rump of a dog. One pigeon man returned to his bale hide after setting up a wing flapper to discover a small boy, holding his gun, pointing it at his stomach and saying 'Stick 'em up!' He was a wise shooter and his gun was unloaded.

The gun should be unloaded when carrying it to and from your shooting place, and certainly when crossing obstacles such as fences and ditches. It should be loaded only when held in your hands and ready to shoot.

Special care must be taken when sharing a hide. I abominate this practice if only because of the danger element, but even as a sporting experience it usually turns out to be fairly unsatisfactory. If you insist on doing it, only one gun should be loaded at once and strict turns must be taken for shooting. The last hide I shared was twenty years ago. My fellow shooter was

Tree hides should be properly maintained

sporting a new-fangled automatic and I was all too conscious of him fiddling with the unfamiliar knobs and levers.

Then some pigeons approached from across the clover field in front and my friend's gun suddenly went off with a deafening explosion. A neat round hole large enough to take a clenched human fist was blown in the straw bale six inches to the left of my knee cap and six inches to the right of my dog's head. My colleague seemed to take the mishap very calmly, I must say, but I lost my stomach for shared hide shooting after that.

Marksmanship The object of this book is to help place the pigeon shooter within range of the birds and to suggest some basic ploys and strategies whereby this might be done. It is not a book on how to shoot straight — for that the reader must look elsewhere and brush up his skills with the clay variety of pigeon.

However, provided the gun fits and the ammunition is suitable and you have set your decoys skilfully enough to present you with your favourite shot, the rest is up to you and your equipment may not be blamed if you make a mess of things. As in most forms of field shooting, most missed pigeons are missed behind, below, or both. Bear this mind and allow good lead and swing at decoyed birds — hence the importance of having enough room at the front opening of the hide to wield the gun properly.

Even the slowest-looking pigeon is still travelling, and oddly enough, these are often the easiest to miss. The sudden crossing snap shot which catches you without time to think, falls every time. However, once you strike a good patch and are able to maintain your concentration you will continue to shoot well. Too few and too irregular chances prevent you from striking a rhythm and make you over-eager and liable to try too hard with the inevitable result of a run of misses.

The big bags of which we hear so much are often built up by a series of rights and lefts or 'double shots'. The trick here is to forget the second barrel for a moment, take all your time and care with the first shot and then start again with your second chance. Quite often a pair of pigeons will approach one behind the other. The trick in this case is to allow the first bird to settle, take the second in the air with the more tightly choked barrel, and clobber the other one with the open pattern as it clatters away. To do this requires a certain amount of self-discipline, but like many other things, it is a knack and, given time, you will become quite good at it.

Sometimes a single bird, too quick for you or unnoticed, will settle among your decoys. Rather than shoot it on the ground — and it is very easy to miss these 'sitters' — leave it alone as the best possible decoy to draw another and, when one comes, act as you do when two come in line astern.

Diversions If a flock builds up away from your decoys, they will draw all new birds to them. They must be put off, not by a shot which might alarm them too much, but by the decoyer showing himself or walking out. If the birds persist in returning to this place, either move your own position there, or hang up a strip of polythene on a stick to prevent them landing there again. The latter is easier, the former, if feasible, might make for a heavier bag.

If you set up and have no shot for an hour, fire your gun into the air. This just might get the birds moving if they have settled within earshot, and start a little flightline to the field you have chosen which will be one they have grown accustomed to using.

Racing pigeons Often when decoying you will find birds other than woodpigeons attracted to your set-up. I have explained already that gamebirds may on no account be shot, and no hares. Vermin such as crows, stoats or rabbits may be taken at any time, for you will be doing the keeper and farmer a good turn. Do not shoot gulls, many of which are protected — it takes a good man to be able to tell the difference.

Know your racing pigeons . . .

Turtle doves and stock doves are also protected, and homing pigeons may *certainly* not be shot. No one could confuse a racer with a woodie. The former is smaller, of different colour, has short wing-beats, a direct line of flight and often flies in a flock of its peers. Usually they will not look at decoys, but come over your head by chance.

These birds are private property, many are very valuable and anyone who shoots one is spoiling the sport of another man, the owner. No game dealer will take them. Feral pigeons (that is, a tame bird now living in the wild and unringed) may come to decoys, as might the residents of a local pigeon loft. A true feral may be shot, but my firm advice is to take no chances.

No protected bird may be shot at any time or under any circumstances.

11 · Seven Pigeon Days

DAY 1

Sometimes one comes across a good, old-fashioned decoying situation when the birds behave like Christians and do some, if not all of the right things, in spite of farmers and their ever more ingenious bird-frighteners.

Back to the spring corn which, once upon a time, was my own favourite decoying ground and which nowadays is so hard to find. I fostered some hopes of a field of late barley sown within easy view of my house. I could keep an eye on it through the bedroom window, taking care lest the glint of my binoculars in the shadow of the curtains put me at risk of accusation by my neighbours of Peeping-Tom-ism. No sooner had a nice lead-in of birds begun to build up, than the farmer — a noted pigeon-hater — had the ten acres turned into a minefield of flappers, kites, gew-gaws, bangers and sirens. Only pigeon made of the sternest stuff, stone deaf or impervious to all man-made frighteners dared to look at it. There were a few such hardy souls which went to prove how quickly some birds have learned to ignore the most sophisticated deterrents, but these were discouraged by the simple expedient of emptying a clip of .22 bullets at them at regular intervals.

So, there was little point in surveying the place further since no pigeon in its right mind could ever feel comfortable there. I had a second string to my bow, only seven acres, but it nestled in the angle of the roosting wood and was the property of a farmer as casual in his approach to crop protection as his neighbour was a pigeon-paranoic. He had the theory that pigeon would never feed in the field that adjoined the roost wood, but would fly out over the most tempting food and travel some distance before dropping in. Accordingly, he drilled the wheat, shut the gate and, with the air of a job well done, returned to the farm to recuperate until spraying time. His yields were never less than those of his more anxious friend down the road.

I have heard that theory before and there is certainly some evidence to support it, but one of the rules of country life is never to say 'never'. These pigeon had not heard the rule and, being so ill-informed, they descended gratefully on the feast spread before them. I had to wait until Saturday until I could go but I was there bright and early with all my equipment, flask and sandwiches for a good, old-fashioned day with the decoys. I travel heavy these days for the modern woodie is a downy bird, not easily deceived like its ancestors, and so all the arts and hardware must be called into play. A few lofters on the stunted ash twenty-five yards down the hedge, a carefully thawed dead bird on a flapper cradle and a mixed squad of artificials and dead birds in a wedge in front of the hide was the plan of the day. The wind blew from behind my left shoulder towards the decoys, so conditions were good: the sun was bright so it was the sort of day to have the pigeon up high, covering the countryside and looking for the companies of grey-cloaked companions on the ground below.

A pair of stockdoves flew in one of their characteristic, lilting circles and alighted with a clatter of wings behind each other out in the field. They have been a protected species, of course, since that curious piece of legislation the Wildlife and Countryside Act 1981. They might at least draw in some pigeon

Setting out a mixed squad of decoys

but they might also draw them in well away from my decoys. Funny how two real live birds have ten times the pull of the best laid squad of stuffed, dead, polymer, plastic or rubber ones. I was still debating what to do, whether to disturb or leave them, when a woodpigeon appeared from nowhere, hovering over my killing area. I snatched the gun, dropped the bird and also took the second one which was coming in unseen behind it and which offered a flaring snap shot across my front.

The stockdoves had departed hurriedly and the sky was empty so I scuttled out to set up the dead birds to add a touch of realism to my display. On my way back to the hide a pigeon came and fluttered round my head, mesmerised by the decoys, looking for a landing place and completely ignoring me; even the wily woodie can act stupidly sometimes. The early morning sport was slow but steady but although I was in an old-fashioned decoying situation, the birds still showed their new-fangled ways by coming in small, quick groups, a dozen at a time, and looking very hard indeed at the decoy pattern. Usually they allowed the breeze to bend their flightline away to safe range and either came round for a second look or departed altogether.

Even so, I had a score of birds by lunchtime. The shooting gave me the chance to give the dog a little reinforcement of his steadiness training — a pigeon or duck hide is the perfect place to do this. The dog is close at hand and may be tethered if necessary; there is no urgency to pick a bird; there is no problem with runners; on a reasonable day, there should be a number of shots, hits and misses, and a sight of passing birds, throughout which the dog may be easily controlled. Retrieves may be carefully selected and kept to a minimum.

After sandwich time, things grew ominously quiet. I managed to pull in one distant passing pigeon by some energetic pulls at the flapper cord. He caught the flick of movement, put on the brakes, cut back in a tight half-circle and came straight in on a long, shallow glide. Just as he pulled up to land, I downed him in a squirt of white feathers so that he fell right in the killing area. That, if you like, was how all well-mannered pigeon used to behave. After that, nothing. I alternately scanned the skies and busied myself tidying up the hide, sorting out my cartridges, improving the camouflage, adding some delicate touches to the decoys, removing tell-tale clumps of white feathers from the field, tuning the action in the flapper, righting an upended lofter — just generally passing the time.

After three hours of this, I was on the point of undoing all my good work and packing up, but then the evening flight home began. Large flocks came high from over the chalk downs to drop into the wood behind me. As usual, one or two of the tail-enders decided that there might just be room in their distended crops for another grain or two. The main flocks passed over but then one and then another of the stragglers began a little lead-in to my decoys so that in the hour before dusk I managed to add a further nine to my score, including one I was particularly proud of which completely ignored the decoys and flew straight and fast over my head like a good driven pheasant. It fell and lodged in the hawthorn and I had to poke it down with a long stick.

To find a flock of old-fashioned pigeon feeding on an old-fashioned, lumpy, spring corn drill is a rare enough event. On the principle of making hay while the sun shines, it is not a chance to be lightly passed over.

DAY 2

Farmers can become paranoid about pigeons on crops. They see twenty and believe they have seen a thousand. Certainly pigeons can ruin crops like soft fruit or growing peas, whereas with drilled seeds the birds are merely taking loose seeds which would not germinate anyway. Unlike a rook which will dig for its food, a pigeon feeds only from the surface.

The farmer of our little rough shoot telephoned more in anger than in sorrow to complain about the pigeon on the rape. As shooting tenant I was supposed to keep the grey army at bay and was failing signally to do so. He had a point, I was bound to admit it. Everyone else's rape was up above knee-height, already bursting into mustard-yellow flowers, but ours held barely the cover for a rabbit — in fact, it took a minute scrutiny of the ground to show that it was a rape field at all. Close study revealed, beneath the charlock and among the chickweed, a few well bitten white stalks, only just identifiable by an 'A' level biologist as members of the genus Brassica.

The farmer expected instant action. 'Will there be someone there today?' he demanded. I did a rapid mental calculation and agreed that there might. I cancelled all my arrangements, lugged out the gear and threw it in the truck. I was peevish, as I felt this to be one of those impossible fields, for we had tried many times for a bag in the winter snows, but found that the birds cleared off at the first shot, never to return that day, leaving the decoyer with a slight touch of frostbite and little else for his pains.

I set out a huge squad of decoys, almost every one I owned — stuffed ones, Shells, Sportplast, wooden antiques, home-made patents, two-wing flappers, a brace of ferals and a plastic crow. They made a goodly show, but I was especially impressed with the moving decoys invented by my friend, that keenest of amateurs, Mr Richardson of the Market Deeping Woodpigeon Club.

These comprised a half-shell stuffed decoy prepared in the · simple method I have described before. In the middle of the underside of the bird is glued a wooden plug like a short section of broomhandle. In this there is a small hole into which fits a leg about 1ft long made of flat, springy steel. The application is simple: jab one end in the ground, fix the other into the decoy and there you have a realistic bird which bobs and weaves in the faintest breath of wind. Mr Richardson has prepared his latest batch of birds in the head-down feeding posture rather than the traditionally alarmed, white neck-patch exposed stance. All in all, they were among the best pigeon decoys of the very many I have seen — and that's some.

A suitably twangy piece of metal should be bent and shaped to fit in the small peg slot of a Shell decoy, either the Shooting Developments lightweight version or the heavier, more rigid polymer-type. These cause the decoy to kick, lift and tilt in the wind, a more eye-catching if slightly less realistic action than that achieved with the rocking peg provided.

This was the first time I had tried them in the field and they gave a natural feel to my squad which, from a distance, looked not dissimilar to the large flock of real birds which had been feeding there when I arrived. I hoped that the pigeon would agree. I settled into a hide which had been built by a previous visitor who was clearly a master of the craft.

A crow decoy to help give more realism to the picture

Built onto a frame of stout hazel rods, tied at all joints with baler twine, enclosed with wide-mesh chicken wire and thatched with reeds, it was a regular four-bedroom, fully detached palace of a hide. There was even a trench dug for the decoyer's feet. The hide had not been used for many weeks, since when some of the strongest gales of the year had sent roof tiles clattering down into the High Street; but that hide, out in an exposed position on the bleak and windy Fen had stood solid, impervious to the worst the storms could do to it.

I draped a net round it and settled myself down. Hares chased and lolloped in front, stopping to nibble. The first pigeon arrived, tilted into the wind and hovered over the killing area, saw something it did not care for and came on to pass over my left shoulder. I snapped it as it passed the left-hand dormer window of the hide and I heard rather than saw it drop on the wheat behind me. That hide was built for hiding in rather than shooting from. The rest of the morning produced a steady trickle and I would have scored more effectively had it not been for the mullion in that portal directly in front of me. Remove it, and the roof would have collapsed.

Several birds which ought by now to be hanging in the shed owe their lives to it, as my confident swing was brought up short by a vertical hazel rod dug in the ground and held firmly in place by a hank of red string. It was frustrating to say the least to pull the trigger and see the pigeon already half a yard ahead of the stationary muzzles. I was just quick enough to bag one as it beat slowly past, completely unaware of my presence. Having once more thumped into the pillar, I managed to hold my fire, quickly withdrew the barrels, poked them equally quickly through the open skylight and loosed off a quick shot somewhere in the right direction. To my complete surprise it worked, for I heard another thump behind me.

Each time I fired the main flock clattered up and away, either on to one of the surrounding fields of wheat or to the heavy plough nearby. This gave me the ideal opportunity to observe closely the behaviour of modern pigeon. Having settled on the resting field and attracted to them all the new arrivals, they began to leapfrog down the field until they were right on the boundary. Then one would hop the dyke and land on the rape; then another and another, then in tens and twenties until the corner of the field was blue with walking, pecking, fluttering shapes, a far more attractive draw, I fear, than the best flappers and rockers ever patented.

At last, an odd rogue pigeon endowed with a greater sense of adventure than the rest, would slide away from the main pack and circle my picture and give me a shot, at which the by now huge flock at the other end roared up and away, back onto the far side of the plough, ready to begin leapfrogging again.

I packed up at tea-time with a nice bag, but even better, with a clear conscience at the thought that the rape might have grown an uninterrupted quarter of an inch thanks to my ministrations.

As a very general rule, rape can take heavy punishment from pigeon and still produce a good crop, provided the birds are kept off in the spring when the new leaf forms.

DAY 3

Late-drilled corn is often worth watching, for pigeons love grain and the occasional late field is a good draw, provided a few seeds have been scattered on the headlands where the drill turns the corner.

This particular year the spring drilling had started at last after weeks of heavy rain. This was 'cuckoo' corn with a vengeance as the cuckoos had arrived at least a week before — the tractors towing drills and harrows purred up and down under fluffy white clouds while they called incessantly from the big wood. 'Cuckoo' corn is held by farmers to have less chance of a good yield than that drilled earlier which has already germinated by the time of the spring sunshine.

After a mild winter in which the soil has not been broken down by the frost, the farmer finds it more difficult to render it into a fine tilth — it tends to remain in obstinate lumps and even with precision drilling a certain amount of seed corn is not covered over. Such a field is a good pigeon field: they will soon find it and mop up the uncovered seeds. On the Fen which has light soil, such circumstances are rare; on heavier upland soil however, even with a savage winter, the preparation of a seed bed is nearly always difficult.

This was just such a field, and although much harrowing and discing had turned the clay into walnut-sized clodlets, the odd grain still showed up yellow and brown in between. The tractor was still in the field as the first birds came lilting out from the wood and established a beach-head in the far corner near the ash tree. Some settled in this tree to have a look round and a sit in the sunshine before dropping from the branches to join their companions down below. It was a 'sitty tree' which would have gladdened the eye of Archie Coats himself.

I was there next day, loaded down with all my stuff, and set up within easy reach of the tree with my decoys showing proudly on the pale clay soil. As usual I had my favourite HH inflatables of which I cannot speak too highly. One or two veterans of fifteen years' service were becoming battle-scarred and holey, but I had stuffed them with foam rubber and although they could no longer be inflated, their appearance in the field was as good as ever.

My nylon stocking net on three poles braced by some stout hawthorn in the hedge provided good camouflage with a background of tender leaves and bursting elderflower buds. I had a five-gallon drum, easily the best if the bulkiest seat, and on this I settled down to await events.

After my last outing when I had got precisely nil I was hardened to long periods of inactivity, but this time a bird was upon me almost immediately. Before I had time to move he settled among the decoys, sat still for a moment and began strutting about. My dilemma as to what to do was resolved by another bird which lofted over the ash, swung round on lazy wings as he saw the decoys and came spiralling down. I rose to my feet, nailed him with the choke and in copy-book style managed to knock down the other bird as he clattered into the air. I nipped out of the hide and set them up with stiff wires under their chins. Good though the HH decoys are, nothing can beat the real thing. This method of dealing with two pigeons, one of which had settled, is the way advocated by the experts but it is all too easy to make a mess of it. You usually miss the second bird, and anticipating this more difficult shot makes you hurry your first, easier chance and quite often you end up missing them both.

I was still scurrying back to the hide when a pigeon settled in the 'sitty tree'. I froze into immobility and then tried to creep back to the gun but it was no good; he was off in a flash. At least this proved that the birds were not 'spooked' but were expecting to come in with confidence. Another one, the same one perhaps, landed in the tree a few minutes later and I felled him in the bramble patch beneath. Next a flock of a dozen flew round, three of them landing in the tree and the rest coming in to the decoys. Another right and left; it was a good start — almost too good to be true. Sure enough, I missed the next two, both pigeons which sat in the tree. A pigeon in a tree is a surprisingly easy thing to miss, a thing I had learned many years ago, but in spite of taking careful aim at the feet each time, both birds flew off with every sign of being unscathed, and I followed them with my eye until they were no more than specks in the distance. I began to wish that I had brought the .22 and a handful of short bullets: it would have been the perfect weapon for such targets.

From then on I concentrated on flying shots over the decoys, and soon the rhythm and 'feel' of the job made things seem easy. In game shooting 'off' days are features of the irregular sportsman's life, and pigeon decoying is no different. On 'on' days you seem relaxed and able to hit anything, whereas perhaps the very next time out you feel you could not hit a barn if you were shut inside it. This was a good day and I found I was killing a regular three out of four, well above my usual average.

Pigeons continued to come in ones, twos and sometimes quite large flocks and my decoy picture of dead birds grew in size and attractiveness. By two in the afternoon the flood became a trickle and finally dried up. I hung on for the best part of another hour during which only two singletons came. No doubt the birds had changed to a fresh field, possibly the clover ley on the other side of the big wood. It might be that they would come back in the evening, but I was satisfied with my tally so far. I gathered the three score and ten of the slain and stumped back to the van.

It was a warm and comfortable feeling to have broken at last a series of poor days' decoying. I reached the van hot and puffing and the cuckoo called again from the thicket. 'Cuckoo corn' may mean bad news for the farmer, but for the pigeon man it can produce good sport.

DAY 4

The photograph on page 13 shows a huge bag of pigeon shot by that expert Cambridgeshire pigeon decoyer, Will Garfit. The bag of 271 was shot over a field of beans, always a pigeon favourite, and on this day, such was the persistence of the birds and Will's good shooting that, at one point, he shot a hundred pigeons in an hour!

I, too, look for beans and spring is a time to seek out a likely field. One Friday in April I realised that pigeon had found the bean field I had in mind. With a dry autumn, the season had been such that there was very little spring corn for them to feed on — it was all winter corn, and had been put in the ground months before. Farmers prefer to get their corn in early so that it has a good start in life, ready to take full advantage of the mild weather of spring. This year had favoured that ploy and the pigeon looked in vain for the drills crawling up and down, and the sacks of seed corn and fertiliser stacked on trailers in the gateways. There were only beans to come, equally beloved of pigeon, but since a far smaller acreage is grown than corn, there is much less for them to attack.

On a somewhat grander scale, fifteen acres of 'tick' or 'horse' beans had gone in at the end of the parish lane. The ground was still a bit lumpy, but the farmer had had to snatch a couple of dry days between showers. Lumpy soil means that the seed is not drilled so economically as it is into a fine tilth, and a certain amount is scattered on the surface. This is what the pigeon likes.

The foraging flocks soon found the field, and flew to an ash tree on the corner whence they trickled down like falling, grey leaves and began marching across the fields, a peck here and a peck there; a few hurrying steps and another stab over there. In a couple of days at that rate and they would clear the lot. Pigeon beaks and crops have a degree of elasticity which allows them to swallow quite large objects: beans and even acorns seem to present them with no problem. Many shooters have recorded pigeon with over fifty acorns in their bulging crops; this greed has a useful side-effect in that this knobbly bag of acorns can act as a flak jacket or shot-deflector.

I lugged all my gear along the hedge to where I judged the flightline crossed and got my hide together. I used a variety of nets so as not to present too uniform a colour. Home-made jobs combined with Leafscreen are a good team, and I use the excellent Shooting Developments' telescopic hide-poles to hold them up. A couple of cord-braces fixed at each end to a hedgerow tree to stabilise the thing and you are well prepared for the day.

For decoys, I also like a mixture of different sorts of artificials but I feel that the dead bird is best of all although it is not always available. Today I had my favourite HH inflatables with a squad of the Shooting Development Shells out to one side. In addition I set up my WAGBI/Semark flapper, a device in which I have come to have great confidence.

Pigeon were circling in ones and twos while I was still out on the field, running the flapper cord to the hide through a chink in the net. It felt like the old, easy days of pigeon shooting, but no doubt they would clear off after the first couple of shots. I had barely settled on my seat and loaded the gun when one came, lilting slowly over my 'picture' and eyeing my landing stage with obvious interest. I stood up deliberately and an almost true cylinder barrel at twenty yards gave him no chance. At my shot, another bird clattered out from the blackthorn hedge to my left where, unbeknown to me he had settled during my preparations. I managed to get him too and he tumbled down, winged, into the dyke. The dog was out in a flash and had him to hand as I was in the act of setting up the first one on a length of stiff wire.

It was to be a good day and, despite my feeling rusty and out of practice, I found that in the first hour I had shot thirty-two pigeon for forty-one cartridges. Then the dreaded complacency set in and while I lost count of the statistics for the second hour, I know full well that my performance slipped. Thus it always is with me: I start well enough, fade and then pick up again later. Other shooters I know start badly and get better through the day as they relax and confidence grows; for others, things are the direct opposite. I expect that we all have our own patterns of performance in a day's decoying.

I need not have put up the wing flapper as the flightline came obliquely over my left shoulder so that the birds saw the decoys the moment they topped the hedge, swung round and beat in to windward to have a closer look. I gave the occasional pull on the string and on two occasions the distant speck of a pigeon, passing far off and almost unseen, half-closed its wings, checked, skimmed round and came whiffling down to provide me with an exhilarating hit. The Shells seemed to be working and they looked attractive enough out on the black, peaty soil. As the numbers of the slain increased, I gradually took in all my artificials until, by lunchtime, I was left with a nice squad of about sixty dead birds and my flapper set out before me.

Obligingly, the pigeon stopped coming at lunchtime allowing me to gulp coffee and snatch a sandwich without panic-stricken moments when, with a scalding cup half-way to the lips, an unexpected customer arrives. This is the usual pattern; so much so that for some, the pouring out of a cup of coffee from a flask has become a talisman which never fails to bring a bird. Today the birds were well-mannered and they gave me a quarter-hour respite. I was in the act of slipping the empty flask back into my bag when the next bird arrived — almost by arrangement, it seemed.

It was teatime when the flight petered out and I was by then trying to guess how many I had down; had I made the elusive hundred? It surely could not be far short of that magic figure. I counted fifty into one sack and an equal number into the second, and after I had dogged out the rest of the hedge we found a dropper, making a total bag of 101. I collected 137 cartridge cases in my rubbish bag after I had taken down the hide. Not every day does it take two trips to cart your bag back to the road. Time was when 100-bird days were not unusual. Today new feeding and behaviour patterns, changes in agriculture and many more pigeon shooters make such an achievement a cause for pride. I wondered how many days of poor bags it would be before I had another.

DAY 5

As the summer grew stale and the corn turned from green to yellow and then to russet my shooting diary shows more decoying exploits on the laid corn. If you keep an eye on the high tension cables which run across the cereal fields, the feeding flocks, invisible in such thick cover when on the ground, will often give themselves away. There they were, sitting up above like a long stave of music, a row of undulating crotchets which might have been penned by Chopin in one of his more extravagant moods. A glance through the binoculars at this nocturne written across the sky showed no more than a flock of pigeon sitting on the power cables. Such a sight is common enough in mid-summer and to the shooter it suggests several things. Firstly, the corn has 'gone down', secondly that the pigeon have found it and thirdly, that there is half a day's decoying there for a resourceful chap.

This year, the lush growing weather had produced long stalks, handsome enough when vertical but easy prey for the violent thunderstorms of early June. More corn than usual was flattened in patches and stripes of haphazard size and distribution. Laid corn, as such, no longer worries the farmer. The pickup reel on his combine can gather barley as flat as a pavement. The problems arise when weeds grow up through the laid crop making it permanently wet and difficult to thresh. The other worry is that pigeon and sparrows, ever fond of green corn, will descend on it in clouds, walk about on it, and strip every available ear.

The shooter, too, is not without his problems, but his are pricks of conscience. They hinge on his views about shooting parent birds which may be feeding youngsters at the nest. Some people are strong-minded enough not to allow the matter to trouble them, but surely the modern shooting man is a more sensitive barometer of wider, ethical considerations than was his grandfather. Those old-timers with their enviably uncomplicated views of life, were not restricted by the strait-jackets of conservation and the environment, by the wider considerations of the shooter and so on which have come along to muddle our thinking. To them, a pigeon was a pigeon, at any time of year and in every circumstance. It was to be fired at on sight and at any range — no questions asked.

So conscience doth make cowards of us all, and we worry more than we used to. Never mind; if the farmer is complaining that his corn is being savaged and that the nation's food supply is in jeopardy, we suppress scruples and sally forth with the clear conscience and avenging ardour of a knight crusader.

This particular Sir Gawain, encumbered not with cuirass, buckler and helmet but floppy hat, kammo shirt and voluminous satchel, and armed, not with lance but his new fowling piece, plodded ungallantly and prosaically through the long grass. The farmer had begged and pleaded for his assistance and he was aware of a job there for the doing.

A convenient elder bush, carefully snicked, and where necessary chopped and rearranged, makes a good hide. The white dinner plates of its flower-heads disguise the inevitable pale flashes of human skin which we all know are such effective bird frighteners. So rich was the vegetation on the bankside that no supplementary net was necessary, and I felt I was well concealed when squatting amid the fragrant June blossoms on a flowery knoll where Oberon himself might have reclined at ease.

The end of a good day on stubble

Showing decoys on corn, even when it is flat, can be a problem. To human and pigeon eyes, the decoys blend too well with the olive and fawn stalks and are too easily overlooked. There are at least two solutions available. The decoyer may elevate his decoys on cradles, long canes, or both, or he may use a wing flapper. He may stretch a piece of netting over the corn and place his decoys on that. An alternative, if he is very lucky, is for him to decoy on the field next door where the cover may be more scant. Pigeon will often use such a field as a resting place where they show up proudly against the dark soil.

Nowadays however such fields are indeed rare, especially in June. The old-fashioned fallow is just that — a thing of the past. Modern fertilisers and efficient farming practices do not permit the luxury of any unproductive fields. Nor was any such godsend on hand to help me, so I settled for my first option and put a tight cluster of static decoys in the middle of a flat patch half the size of a tennis court, and dotted some HH inflatables stuffed with foam rubber on canes round the edge. When in position, each of these was just above the ears of the standing barley so as to be visible at the optimum distance.

My flapper I put on a stout pole at the same height, with a long skewer stuck in the ground to guide the line and eliminate the leverage which otherwise would pull down the contraption every time I attempted to flap. Birds were clattering out of the ash tree and arrowing high across the grey sky as I went about my business; a further dozen sprang from the muck-heap by the gate. Such signs of general pigeon traffic in my area gave me cause for hope as I nestled into my bower, but I have been caught out too often before to allow wild optimism to hold sway.

A quick queue of early customers gave me a dozen shots in a few minutes. The art of shooting over standing corn is to drop your dead birds in a specific area, as small and as near the decoys as possible. It rather defeats the object of the exercise if you have to trample down more standing corn than you protect as you collect the slain. A dog is not the answer in June. Gamebirds are at peak hatching time and, while your shots will not unduly disturb them, you cannot risk a gundog prancing around where eggs may be on the point of chipping. As a callow youth, I had a bad experience with a grey partridge nest. A galumphing labrador was sent to fetch a pigeon from a hedge bottom; he thrust his nose at a hen bird which gamely flew back in his face. I caught a glimpse of her nest and saw egg shells and new chicks in a jumble as I bellowed the dog to heel and quickly backed away. So much for nesting gamebirds having no scent! I learned a lesson that day I have not forgotten.

The cornfield pigeon shooter must use self-restraint and fire only at birds he can kill cleanly and pick up without damaging the crop further. This means limited bags and some frustrating moments as birds pass you by in easy range but over the wrong place. By waiting until my first few clients were virtually hovering over the decoys, I was able to drop nine of them into a tidy pile. These I set up with wings and tails spread to supplement the decoys and show a concentrated pocket of black, grey and white. The usual rules of decoy spacing may be forgotten in a small patch of laid corn. Squeeze into it as many as you possibly can.

I gave the flapper a few desultory pulls, but it was not really necessary and I worked it as much for the pleasure of seeing it in action as for a belief in its magnetic powers. It certainly added a touch of realism and, who knows, it may have attracted pigeon unseen by me, with its beguiling flash of white — now you see it, now you don't — which is the key to successful flapping.

The early rush was, of course, followed by a lull. Then one came, then another, then five, then one, and so on for about half-an-hour. This is the ideal way for decoyed pigeon or wildfowl to present themselves, in small numbers rather than in bewildering large flocks which you scare each time you fire.

There was the ripe scent of bruised grass in my nostrils. The afternoon grew drowsy, the trickle of pigeon ceased and, instead, they sat up in the dead elms on the far side of the field and appeared to go to sleep. Such fickle conduct by modern pigeon has been so frequently observed as to be no longer worthy of comment. Even the flapper failed to tempt them. The wind grew chill, my position seemed suddenly cramped and uncomfortable. No birds came.

I took my twenty-eight pigeon, shouldered my carefully balanced load of equipment and waded through the meadow-sweet back to the farmyard and the waiting car.

It was no day for the record books, but many a time and often have I come home with less.

DAY 6

I have warned of the problems of shared hides and I feel only slightly less keenly about shared fields, unless it is with someone you know and trust. An amateur can spoil your shooting at the other end of the field he occupies. This cautionary tale will be familiar to any pigeon man who has waited long hours on overshot rape fields — a once good rape field becomes a focal point for every pigeon man in the area: but only the farmer ends the day pleased!

There had certainly been, at one time, pigeon on this particular field. During the week they had been in there in lines and clumps up and down the whole length of the fifty acres. It was admittedly a huge field, old stubble, the stalks silvery grey and the undersown clover showing boldly through. In the hard winter weather it had been a 'duffer's' field as the birds had attacked rapaciously those wide, green swathes whenever snow permitted. Some good bags were made in those early days, nothing spectacular but forties, fifties and sixties being reported most weeks.

Now the glut had passed and as the milder days came along the pigeon man wandered further afield, working the rape, the chickweed and finally the spring drillings. The fifty acres became neglected and the birds discovered it once more. Farmer Geoffrey phoned on Friday to report that pigeons were all over the big field. The following day was free so I decided to give it a try, now that the other gunners had gone. I have an aversion to pigeon decoying in crowds; to me it is a solitary sport and another chap can be distracting and can disturb your carefully researched flightline.

I reached the field by 10.00am, quite time enough for a day's pigeon shooting. On the way I met the policeman on patrol for wandering coursers. These gentry are a real menace in our parts and only vigilant police and tough keepers can keep them at bay. That delay, brief though it was, cost me my place, for when I arrived another heavily loaded pigeon shooter was approaching the bale hide which I had already earmarked for myself. My heart sank but I stopped and glassed the field and watched the usurper setting out his decoys.

I drove along the road to the next hide and saw yet another car parked by the far hedge and a hundred yards further on, a distinct rectangular dark blob of 'kammo' netting. I was inclined to go home there and then, but the second bale hide was untenanted and I had come quite a long way, so I settled for third choice of position and decided to give it a couple of hours and see what happened.

I set out a dozen HH inflatable decoys; my word but they showed up handsomely on that stubble, set on the sunny side of a long slope in the middle of the field. My Semark flapper was in its operational position and I had a stuffed bird on a long stick. A lone crow set a little apart added what I hoped would be both a touch of realism and an eyecatcher. A big field and wary birds need not only the best decoys but a touch of variety and a big squad if you are to have much chance of success.

The bale hide was a slum. It had been occupied by other shooters during the winter but still, it stood solidly enough. Inside it was a mess. The floor was a mudbath pounded by many a Wellington. It was littered with a mosaic of cartridge cases of almost every bore and every colour — they lay pressed into the mud or lodged in chinks in the bales. The bale seat was saturated with rain, and dank and mouldy. It was scattered with old white pigeon feathers and behind it lay a pigeon carcase, half-consumed by rats; it had doubtless been overlooked by a previous occupant. One or two empty cigarette packets gave an apt finishing touch to the squalid scene.

I settled down quickly, spreading a sack and a polythene bag over the wet seat as a guard against that unpleasant condition with which those used to sitting in set places are often afflicted.

There was a distant shot from the man in the far bales and I peeped under my net in time to see a bunch of birds twisting and scattering in alarm but coming my way. A large, black labrador bounded out of the hide, rushed thirty yards or so and returned slowly with something in his mouth. The birds came on but soon I could tell that they would give me no chance after all. They went on, rising and falling to give number two gun in the hedge a quick chance, the results of which I could not discern; he had no dog.

This happened twice more while the dog and I peered out in gloomy unemployment. Hares chased each other and stopped short to nibble the greenery. Overhead an exultation (perfect word) of skylarks sang to the first real sunshine they had seen for weeks. I tried the old dodge of opening my sandwiches, pretending to Fate that my attention was wavering from the job in hand. This time she was not fooled. There was another shot from the far bales. I tried again, this time with a mug of hot soup — hardly ever known to fail, but today even this stratagem did not send me the bird I wanted.

They had simply cleared off to other pastures. The whole countryside was a patchwork quilt of suitable feeding fields and they were in no way committed to the fifty acres.

An hour passed; another was almost gone, and then a small group of birds came wavering towards me, looking dark against the pale field and powder-blue sky. They were not intending to land and looked 'spooky' so I fired at the tail-ender as they passed; he staggered but recovered, separated from the rest and went soaring away into the distance. He crossed the road still climbing and over another large field and when he was no more than a distant speck he came tumbling down to earth. It was too far for me to go, the line too indistinct with that hedge in the way and the cover too thick for it to be worthwhile my going to search for him. It was all the luck I could expect on a day as ill-fated as this and when I missed the next, easier bird with both barrels I could sense the silent gunners in hedge and bales noting my performance with a distinct coolness.

Those were the last shots I fired. A further hour passed and I began to consider packing up. The man in the other bales thought likewise for I saw his ant-like figure coming out with a sack in tow. He bent down and put something into it, moved on a few paces and repeated the process ten ... eleven ... twelve ... he did this fourteen times — not many for a morning's decoying perhaps, but good enough on an impossible day and fourteen more than I had to show.

The man in the hedge turned out to be from the Cambridgeshire Fieldsports Association and he had half-a-dozen. He too was drawing stumps. We stood on the roadside commiserating with each other when another car drew up and yet a fourth pigeon shooter emerged, hauled out his gear and rushed out to the bales I had lately occupied — eager and panting to get started. Farmer Geoffrey had evidently got his team of human scarecrows well organised.

I drove slowly down the road to the village inn; on the way I passed a small van coming the other way. On its roof-rack were rolls of netting and hide poles in bundles. A dog sat on the passenger seat and the driver's face wore an expression of eager expectation. My dog Kenzie and I knew exactly where he was going. We permitted ourselves a sardonic smile.

DAY 7

On the seventh day I did not rest, but pressed on regardless and I relate this last little cameo to show that things might not always seem promising when you set out, but don't ever fail to go because of the weather. Cold weather shooting is a tough job and one for the patient and resilient. However, always turn out if you think there is a chance — only by experiencing bad days will you learn to take advantage of the good ones. Nowadays especially, you would expect a number of bad before you could qualify for one of the good.

There are advantages and drawbacks to pigeon shooting in winter. In some ways the sport is more like wildfowling as, growing colder by the minute, you crouch in a hide. It is a far cry from lounging indolently in the shade of an elder bush by a stubble on a bee-buzzing August afternoon. You will need to wrap up well, with plenty of layers of warm clothes, a hand-warmer or two, balaclava helmet and other Arctic wear. Waiting in a hide, trying to keep still for a long period, means that the body-heat gradually leaks away and a cold shooter is often a bad shooter. It may be necessary to come out of the hide during a lull and stamp up and down, violently flapping the arms in order to restore the circulation.

Another difference is the hide. The usual dark-green and brown camouflage netting is far too conspicuous against the bleached grass and generally pale hues of winter and there is a shortage of foliage and natural materials to make a natural hide. A patchwork quilt of old sacks, bundles of dead sticks or, best of all, a pale Grassscreen will be pressed into service by the imaginative. Sparse vegetation also means that your static ground decoys will show up proudly, but it is worth remembering that on snow, heavy hoar frost or in tall kale or rape, decoys do not seem to be seen easily by pigeon eyes: even a wing-flapper loses its magic.

Hides that were deadly in summer can often be a disappointment come winter

On the credit side, you will be one of the few decoyers out: the rest of them will be snug indoors or out in pursuit of what they consider to be nobler quarry. Also, the birds will tend to be more hungry and will feed hard during the short hours of daylight. I write now of pigeon which are not suffering from a long spell of snow and frost when the food supply is locked away and they quickly lose condition. In fact, pigeon in early winter are often in surprisingly good trim and as fat as butter.

Bearing my own advice in mind, I muffled myself heavily in layers of quilted coats until I resembled one, if not both, of the Michelin twins: it was not ideal for swift shooting, but at least I would not suffer from exposure. Lover as I am of the English countryside in all its moods, a dank December day is not the time to see it at its best. Just for once I fell prey to the guilty thought that, were I a man of means, I would summon up my private helicopter, float out to the nearest airport and, with a clean shirt and a toothbrush as luggage, jet out to some remote sub-tropical spot. Wishful thinking comes easily with a 50lb rucksack on your back and the icy sludge of Fen mud creeping further up your boots with every step. It was not to be, and no magic chopper came whirring down to whisk me away to the sunshine.

I pushed such traitorous thoughts to the back of my mind and set up a squad of twenty HH decoys on the old stubble, twenty yards from a thick thorn hedge. I chopped away at some dead hawthorn, getting well pricked for my troubles, but I managed to erect a rough thorn boma, or truncated wigwam which I clad in a skirt made of my lightest shade of hide netting. Getting it off again at the end took rather longer. Seated comfortably therein, I pulled my drapes firmly about me and gazed out of my 'picture'. Three pheasants came out from the stand of maize on the next field and strutted about. The dreary gloom of the winter's day had turned even the cock's glorious colours to drab fustian.

Then, wondrous to relate, a pigeon came and settled on the ash tree, thirty yards away. Recalling the advice I first read in a Min of Ag pamphlet back in the fifties, I took careful aim at its feet and fired the choke barrel. Having followed this advice regularly for thirty years I knew exactly what to expect, so was not surprised when the bird went clattering away, apparently untouched, to fly strongly across the river and out of sight.

My peripheral vision of earlier weeks had not played me false for birds did start dropping in, circling high above like wheeling buzzards in diminishing circles — one moment dots in the sky and the next hovering over the decoys. These hoverers can be as hard to hit as birds sitting in ash trees, but my blood was up — cold, but up — and I got the first five without a miss. Then a flock came and three fell out; too good to be true and I counted my blessings and my birds as I restored my circulation by scampering out to set them up.

The rest of the afternoon was a miracle, a recollection of a good day back in the '50s when the ill-advised pamphlet was written. Birds came in boldly in a steady trickle and while my opening average was far too good to last, I killed more than I missed, ending the day with sixty-two birds in the bag and a quiet glow of pride in my thermolactycally encased bosom.

When it was all over, I trudged back to the homes of civilised men and a warming dram with all thoughts of tropical climes and suchlike nonsense vanished like a summer mist.

The diary records many other days of pigeon shooting and wildfowling when 'I nearly didn't go', days when I turned out in the end and found myself enjoying superb sport.

'You've cooked the decoy!' A young bride's first encounter with colomba palumbus *might not be a complete success . . .*

12 · Pigeon Pie

This chapter by Angela Humphreys, 'Guidwife' of Sporting
Gun *magazine and author of* Game Cookery
(David & Charles)

Pigeon has featured on menus in British households for several centuries. During the sixteenth century large country houses bred pigeons for food. The Star Chamber Accounts record the price of pigeons, distinguishing between the tame or 'house' pigeon and the wild variety. From 1519–35 the price was 1d each or 10d a dozen. By 1590 the price had risen to 2½d for a wild bird. By 1605 the price was up to 8d a bird and by 1635 they cost 14s a dozen. Two-and-a-half centuries later, when they were a favourite on Victorian and Edwardian tables, the price was still in the region of 1s each.

Today the price of birds fluctuates according to their condition and availability, but it is fair to say that they are cheaper to buy today than a century ago, especially if bought from a game dealer. Supermarket prices tend to be inflated with a whole, oven-ready pigeon selling for around 85p each. It makes economic sense for the sporting wife to use all the pigeons her husband brings home to provide cheap, nutritious family and gourmet meals throughout the year.

Concerned as we all should be with healthy eating, the pigeon — along with all game birds, wildfowl, hares, rabbit and venison — has a much lower proportion of fat than pork, beef or lamb and what fat there is, is relatively high in healthy polyunsaturates.

Pigeons do not need to be hung like game but should not be left in a bag or a jumbled heap. Lay them out on shady concrete or hang them by the neck in a cool place. If you are not going to prepare them immediately for cooking or freezing, it is a good idea to remove the crop to prevent decomposing food-stuff spoiling the meat.

Pigeon plucking is best done outdoors

Pigeons are very easy birds to prepare. If they are young and are to be roasted either whole or boned, then pluck the whole bird, but cut off the wings at the first joint as they have very little meat on them. Remove the head and feet. From the neck end remove the crop and windpipe. Lift up the pointed end of the breastbone and make an incision above the vent and draw out the entrails. Reserve the liver, heart and gizzard for stock.

Many recipes require only the breast meat, in which case there is no need to pluck the whole bird. The legs are worth keeping to use in casseroles or pâté. Pluck the feathers from the breast area and the legs. Remove the legs close to the body with a sharp knife and cut off the feet with kitchen scissors. Lift up the pointed end of the breastbone and cut up each side of the body to the wings. Cut through the collarbones with stout scissors and lift off the complete breast. Finally, remove the skin from the meat. The liver, heart and gizzard may be used for stock or fed (cooked, not raw) to the dog. If you have ferrets they will appreciate the rest of the bird so nothing is wasted.

THE GREENHILL METHOD

It is not often in this life that someone comes up with a brilliant new idea which is more simple, quick and efficient than the best of the existing systems. When this can be said of such an ancient practice as the preparation of game for the table, the occurrence becomes even more worthy of note.

Fed up with the clouds of feathers caused by plucking, and then even with the much quicker method of part skinning, part cutting, since this resulted in the best portions of the bird being removed, Ron Greenhill evolved his own process which produced an oven-ready bird in less than a minute. Actually, even to fully pluck a woodpigeon can be reduced to a minute, as has been demonstrated often enough at Game Fairs during the BASC pigeon plucking contests — but even the most swiftly-plucked bird needs to be gutted and cleaned and no matter how good you are, that is a job which cannot be hurried.

The Greenhill method combines the two, and in a few deft movements gives you all the breast meat, on the bone, and ready for the oven. My young son did it in forty seconds at his *first attempt*, so I write of what I know. No knife or scissors are required. This is what you do:

1 Break each wing as close to the body as possible. The wing may twist at the first joint especially if your hands are not strong, but do not worry: just screw the wing round and round, and in about three turns it will break off clean.
2 Holding the bird head down over a bucket, tear off the crop, the bag of skin at the base of the neck above the bulk of the massive breast muscles. Sometimes the head will come off too, but do not worry.
3 Insert both thumbs into the cavity you have just created at the base of the neck and, as if breaking open a tough bread roll or opening a crab, break the bird in half along its length. This is easier than it sounds and requires comparatively little strength.
4 Break the bird wide open from crop to vent, continue the process by peeling off from the rear the thick breast skin with feathers attached. You are left with the backbone, ribs, entrails, legs, tail and breast skin in one hand and in the other the breastbone and all the meat with a few loose feathers adhering to it.
5 Pick off the loose feathers and drop the clean meat into a bowl of water for a short soaking.

I could have prepared six birds in the time is has taken me to write this page. This simple method makes it possible to prepare a large bag of pigeons in a very short time and the surplus should be stored in polythene bags in the deep freeze.

For quick-cooking recipes in which the meat is to be grilled or fried there is no need to remove the whole breastbone. With a sharp knife make a 2in (5cm) cut down the centre of the breast above the bone and peel off the skin and feathers. Then slice the meat off either side of the breast.

Pigeons will keep well in the deep freeze for up to nine months. They may be frozen whole or in family-sized packs, usually allowing one bird per person.

The illustrations on pp174–5 and 176 show the Ron Greenhill method of pigeon preparation: oven-ready in 40 seconds

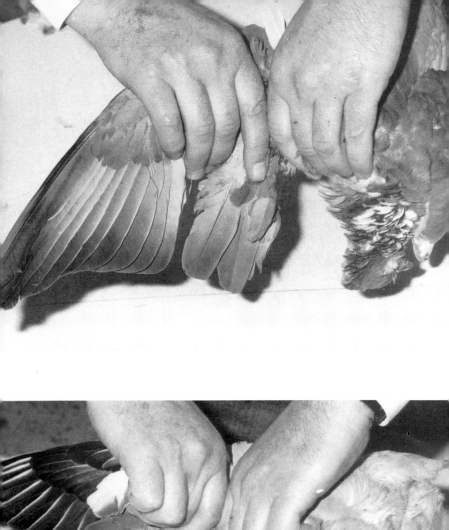

There are many ways of serving pigeon. Although Isobella Beeton lists merely 'four ways with pigeon' — broiled, roasted, stewed or baked in a pie — *Cassell's Dictionary of Cookery*, popular in Edwardian times, contains no less than forty-three recipes.

Squabs or young pigeons, best between August and October, are tender and succulent and may be plainly roasted or stuffed with a herb-flavoured cream cheese, sausagemeat, fruit or nut stuffing. Cover the breasts with streaky bacon rashers to prevent the meat from drying out and becoming tough. Pigeon breasts may be cooked quickly like steak and served while still faintly pink. Older birds require a longer cooking method and may be marinated first in wine, oil and herbs.

They may be pot-roasted, casseroled with vegetables, fruits and nuts, or served as a pie or pudding. They also make delicious pâté and terrines.

Pigeons may be successfully cooked in a microwave oven. Either use the lowest power level or on A8 if you have an automatic sensor.

The flavour of a pigeon stew is improved if cooked one day

and reheated the next. For casseroles and stews I prefer to cook pigeons on the bone, then remove and slice the meat, return it to the casserole and reheat for at least another thirty minutes, adding any last minute ingredients such as mushrooms, nuts, yoghurt, cream or a fruit jelly.

BOURSIN PIGEON
(Serves 2)

Only young pigeons or squabs are tender enough to roast. Having very little natural fat they tend to dry out easily. This may be overcome by wrapping bacon rashers round the birds and using a moist stuffing in the body cavity. This may be sausagemeat, herbs and breadcrumbs or simply chopped apple, onion or orange. Here a herb and garlic cream cheese is used. This gives 'bite' to the sauce without masking the flavour of the pigeons.

2 young pigeons	3 tbsp red wine
100g/4oz Boursin cheese	Watercress to garnish
4 rashers streaky bacon	

Place half of the cheese in the body cavity of each pigeon. Truss the birds and wrap two rashers of bacon round each breast. Cook in a moderately hot oven 190°C/375°F, gas mark 5, for 45 minutes.

Roll the bacon rashers. Cut each pigeon in half using game shears or kitchen scissors. Scoop out any remaining cheese and add to the pan juices.

Arrange the pigeons and bacon onto a serving dish and keep hot.

Add the wine to the pan juices and heat through gently, stirring to blend in the cheese. Do not allow the sauce to boil. Pour the sauce over the pigeons and garnish with watercress.

Serve immediately.

BONED PIGEON ROULÉ
(Serves 4)

Here young pigeons are boned completely, stuffed and rolled. This is a more unusual way to serve pigeon and well worth the effort for a special occasion. Allow one bird per person.

4 young pigeons, boned (see method)	4 rashers streaky bacon
225g/8oz sausagemeat	Parsley for garnish
2 tbsp mixed herbs	Redcurrant or elderberry jelly

To bone the pigeons: With a small, sharp knife cut off the wings close to the body, and the legs below the drumsticks. Cut the skin down the back of the pigeon. Scrape the flesh from the carcase working towards the leg. When you reach the thigh joint, break it and scrape the meat from the leg bones and remove them. Repeat with the other leg.

Work off the flesh from either side of the breast bone and lift out the carcase. Be very careful not to split the skin. Use the bones for stock.

Lay the bird skin side down. Mix the herbs with the sausagemeat and place the stuffing on the pigeon meat. Roll the meat and secure with fine string or tough cotton.

Wrap a rasher of bacon round each pigeon. Place the birds in a shallow casserole and cook in a moderate oven 180°C/350°F, gas mark 4, for one hour. Serve with a fruit jelly.

PIGEON À L'ORANGE
(Serves 4)

Marinating pigeons in red wine and olive oil helps to tenderise older birds. The contrasting flavour and texture of oranges and walnuts complement the dark, richly flavoured meat.

4 whole pigeon breasts	Salt and pepper
150ml/¼pt pure orange juice	
100g/4oz mushrooms, sliced	*For the marinade*
50g/2oz walnuts, halved	150ml/¼pt red wine
2 oranges	1 tbsp olive oil
1 tbsp redcurrant jelly	Sprig of fresh sage and thyme
1 tbsp flour	

Place the pigeons breast down in the marinade and leave in the refrigerator for 48 hours. In a flameproof casserole, blend the flour with the orange juice, add the marinade and slowly bring to the boil, stirring all the time.

Add the pigeon breasts to the casserole. Cover and cook in a moderate oven 160°C/325°F, gas mark 3, for 1½ hours.

Peel the oranges and break into segments, removing any pith and pips. Remove the meat from the casserole. Stir in the fruit jelly, and add the orange segments, mushrooms and walnuts.

Cut the meat from the breastbone and slice each half into 3-4 pieces. Return the meat to the casserole and cook for a further 30 minutes.

Serve with a green vegetable, baked potatoes and sour cream.

PIGEON PARCELS
(Serves 4-8)

Young pigeons may be successfully cooked on a barbecue for an Indian summer al fresco meal. This recipe uses elderberry jelly, but cranberry, redcurrant or crab apple are equally good.

4 pigeons, split in half
8 rashers streaky bacon

8 tbsp elderberry jelly
Salt and pepper

Wrap a rasher of bacon round each pigeon half, and place in the centre of a square of foil. Place one tablespoon of elderberry jelly on top and carefully seal the foil parcel.

Cook on a hot barbecue for about 15 minutes.

Serve with crusty bread and salads.

CHINESE PIGEON
(Serves 4)

A very easy recipe for the cook in a hurry. Prepare the sauce, all the vegetables and slice the meat before starting to cook. Use a wok if you have one, as it is the best shape for quick stir-frying and ensures an even distribution of heat.

4 whole pigeon breasts
2 leeks, sliced
1 red pepper, deseeded
  and chopped
225g/8oz mushrooms, sliced

2 tbsp sunflower oil
4 tbsp red wine
1 tbsp mushroom ketchup
1 tbsp soy sauce
2 tbsp tomato paste

Mix together the wine, ketchup, soy sauce and tomato paste.

Remove the pigeon meat from the breastbone and cut into

small shreds. Heat 1 tbsp oil in a wok or large frying pan. Add the prepared vegetables and stir-fry for three minutes. Push to the side of the wok.

Add the rest of the oil and stir-fry the pigeon meat for about five minutes so that the pigeon is just cooked through. Do not overcook or the meat will become tough.

Mix the vegetables with the meat and add the sauce stirring while it heats through.

Serve immediately with rice or pasta and a beansprout and diced cucumber salad tossed in a light dressing.

PIGEON HOT POT
(Serves 4)

Pigeon breasts are marinated in beer, baked with a selection of winter vegetables and topped with sliced potatoes to make a complete family meal.

4 whole pigeon breasts	2 sticks celery, chopped
450g/1lb carrots, peeled and sliced	300ml/½pt stock
	2 tbsp flour
450g/1lb parsnips, peeled and sliced	25g/1oz butter or margarine
450g/1lb leeks, cleaned and sliced	*For the marinade*
	300ml/½pt beer
900g/2lb potatoes, peeled and sliced	1 small onion, finely sliced
	Sprig of rosemary
410g/14½oz tin tomatoes	

Place the pigeons in a large casserole. Add the beer, onion and rosemary. Cover and leave in a cool place for 24 hours.

Blend the flour with the stock and add to the casserole together with the carrots, parsnips, leeks, celery, tomatoes, salt and pepper.

Cover and cook in a moderate oven 180°C/350°F, gas mark 4, for 1½ hours.

Remove the pigeon breasts and when cool enough to handle, slice the meat from the bone. Return to the casserole.

Cover the top with sliced potato, sprinkle with salt and pepper, cover and cook for a further one hour.

Increase the temperature of the oven to 220°C/425°F, gas mark 7.

Remove the lid of the casserole, dot the potatoes with the butter, and bake uncovered for a further 15 minutes or until the potatoes are brown.

CRANBERRY PIGEONS
(Serves 4-6)
A recipe for the microwave oven

The slow cooking necessary to produce a tender, well-flavoured pigeon casserole is possible in most microwave ovens. The advantage of the microwave is not necessarily the speed, as the tender results can only be achieved by a long, slow cooking method, but the saving of energy and the simplicity of preparation, cooking the day before then refrigerating and re-heating, will all help to develop the flavour as in conventional cooking.

6 whole pigeon breasts and legs	100g/4oz mushrooms, sliced
300ml/¹/₂pt red wine	2 tbsp flour
300ml/¹/₂pt good stock	2 tbsp cranberry sauce
1 small onion, chopped	Bay leaf
1 green pepper, deseeded and chopped	Sprig of thyme
1 red pepper, deseeded and chopped	Salt and black pepper

Place the legs and pigeon breasts, flesh side down, in a large microwave proof casserole.

Add the wine, herbs, chopped onion, peppers, salt and pepper. Blend the flour with the stock and add to the casserole. The liquid should cover the meat.

Cook on a low power setting for 1 hour 20 mins or on A8 automatic setting.

When cool, remove the meat from the breastbone and cut into slices. Add the sliced mushrooms, and stir in the cranberry sauce. Adjust the seasoning if necessary.

Reheat on medium power for 20 minutes or on A1 automatic setting.

PIGEON NORMANDE
(Serves 4)

Pigeon breasts are marinated in white wine, then cooked slowly with dessert apples. The apples are puréed and blended with fromage frais to make a smooth creamy sauce.

4 whole pigeon breasts	450g/1lb dessert apples, peeled and sliced
150ml/¹/₄pt white wine	
1 small onion, finely chopped	2 tbsp fromage frais
Bay leaf	Salt and pepper
150ml/¹/₄pt game stock	

Place the wine, chopped onion and bay leaf in a flameproof casserole, add the pigeon breasts, meat side down, and marinate for 24 hours.

Add the apples and stock, cover and cook in a moderate oven 160°C/325°F, gas mark 3, for 1½–2 hours or until the pigeons are tender.

Remove the pigeons from the casserole. The meat may be removed from the bone at this stage. Pass the apples and onion through a sieve or liquidise to a purée. Return the purée to the casserole and stir in the fromage frais. Add the meat and reheat very gently on top of the cooker. Season if necessary.

Spring cabbage makes a delicious accompaniment to pigeon especially when cooked in a little butter with chopped bacon, grated onion and a pinch of nutmeg.

PICHON AGRIDULCE
(Serves 4)

In this Spanish recipe, the addition of a small amount of chocolate gives a smooth rich flavour to this sweet and sour sauce to accompany pigeon.

4 whole pigeon breasts	Salt and pepper
8 sweet pickled onions	25g/1oz butter
8 cloves	25g/1oz dark chocolate
4 tbsp red wine vinegar	1 tsp cornflour
150ml/¼pt red wine	Parsley for garnish
2 tbsp flour	

Coat the pigeon breasts in the seasoned flour.

Heat the butter in a flame-proof casserole, add the pigeons and cook until brown.

Stick a clove into each pickled onion and add to the casserole with the wine and wine vinegar. Bring to the boil and simmer gently for 1–1½ hours or until the pigeons are tender.

Remove the pigeons from the casserole.

Blend the cornflour with a little cold water then add to the sauce, stirring until thickened. Add the chocolate and stir until melted. Adjust the seasoning if necessary.

Remove the meat from the breastbone, cut into slices and return to the casserole. Heat through gently.

Arrange the pigeon meat on a serving dish and pour over the sauce. Decorate with the onions and parsley.

Serve immediately with freshly cooked buttered noodles.

PIGEON PIE
(Serves 4)

This pie packed with meat, hard-boiled eggs and mushrooms makes a nourishing meal for a winter's evening. Cook the meat on the bone as this will help to enrich the gravy. The breastbones may be discarded before filling the pie dish.

4 whole pigeon breasts	1 tsp dried mixed herbs
4 hard-boiled eggs, sliced	25g/1oz flour
100g/4oz mushrooms, sliced	1 tbsp redcurrant jelly
1 small onion, finely chopped	Salt and pepper
150ml/1/4pt red wine	225g/8oz flaky pastry
150ml/1/4pt stock	1 egg, beaten

Place pigeon breasts, chopped onion, wine and stock into a saucepan, bring to the boil and simmer gently for 1 1/2 hours. When cool remove the pigeon breasts. Cut the meat from the bone and slice each breast half into 3–4 slices. Place a funnel in the centre of a pie dish.

Add the meat, sliced hard-boiled eggs and mushrooms. Thicken the stock with the flour, add the redcurrant jelly and salt and pepper to taste. Pour the gravy into the pie dish, cover with flaky pastry and brush with beaten egg. Bake in a hot oven 220°C/425°F, gas mark 7, for 40 minutes or until the pastry is golden brown.

Serve with creamed potatoes and Brussels sprouts.

PIGEON PÂTÉ
(Serves 6)

A smooth, rich pâté which is easy to make especially if you have a food processor. Serve with toast as a first course, or with salads and French bread for a light lunch or picnic meal.

4 whole pigeon breasts	2 tbsp single cream
100g/4oz streaky bacon	1/2 tsp dried sage
50g/2oz butter	Pinch nutmeg
1 small onion, chopped	Black pepper
2 tbsp brandy	Parsley for garnish

Fry the bacon and onion in 25g/1oz melted butter until soft but not browned. Remove from the pan.

Cut the pigeon meat into small pieces. Melt the rest of the butter and cook the pigeon until just cooked through. This will take about 5 minutes.

Place the pigeon meat, bacon and onion in a food processor or liquidiser. Add the brandy, cream, dried sage, nutmeg, pepper and any juices left in the pan, and mix until smooth.

Turn into a dish and chill.

Decorate with parsley before serving.

JELLIED PIGEONS
(Serves 6)

Glazed with jellied stock, pigeon, ham and hard-boiled eggs make an attractive cold dish to serve as a first course or as part of a buffet meal.

4 whole pigeon breasts	1 level tbsp powdered gelatine
225g/8oz cooked ham, diced	Bay leaf
2 hard-boiled eggs, sliced into rings	Watercress or celery leaves for garnish
450ml/³/₄pt stock	Tomato wedges and cucumber slices

Place the pigeon breasts in a saucepan with the stock and bay leaf. Simmer for 1½ hours. When cool, remove the meat from the bone and cut into thin slices. Mix with the diced ham. Dissolve the gelatine in the remaining stock. Wet a 900ml/1½ pint plastic ring mould and line the base and sides with the egg slices. Add the meat mixture and pour over the jellied stock. Leave to set, then chill in the refrigerator.

Just before serving, unmould onto a plate, decorate with the tomato and cucumber and fill the centre with watercress or celery leaves.

13 · Finale

The intention of this book has been to help to put one or two more pigeons in various bags up and down the land, and if it does no more, I will be satisfied.

I have gained much pleasure from watching my two sons, David and Peter, becoming quite competent pigeon shooters. Many days they failed and as chauffeur I collected them at the end of the day and noticed the old errors: poor hide, carelessly placed decoys, wrong place, not enough time spent on reconnaisance — they committed all the classic mistakes. Rather than make it easy and deliver a long lecture each time, I was able by a hint here and a word there to help them to recognise where they were going wrong.

Then, by degrees, the blank days became less frequent and they had discovered the delights of finding out for themselves, learning lessons the hard way and seeing their success growing.

It is no easy sport and I have been at pains in the foregoing chapters to point out that the 1990 pigeon is not the pushover of its predecessor in 1960.

I hope that these few thoughts, recollections and scraps of advice will do for the reader what they have done for David and Peter: if they have given him some satisfaction in what is still a fascinating, challenging and exciting sport, the effort will have been worthwhile.

Index

Figures in *italic* denote illustrations

David & Charles' Fieldsports and Fishing Titles

The Angling Times Book of Coarse Fishing · Allan Haines and
  Mac Campbell
Beagling · J. C. Jeremy Hobson
The Best of Dick Walker's Coarse Fishing · Dick Walker
Fishing from my Angle · Tales by Cyril Holbrook
Fly Dressing I · David J. Collyer
Fly Dressing II · David J. Collyer
Fly-tying Methods · Darrel Martin
Fowler in the Wild · Eric Begbie
Fox Hunting · The Duke of Beaufort
Game Cookery · Angela Humphreys
Gamekeeper · John Foyster and Keith Proud
Good Shooting · J. E. M. Ruffer
The Great Shoots · Brian P. Martin
Ken Whitehead's Pike Fishing · Kenneth Whitehead
Hunter's Fen · John Humphreys
Purdey's: The Guns and the Family · Richard Beaumont
Shotgun · Macdonald Hastings
Sporting Birds of the British Isles · Brian P. Martin
Sporting Gun · James Douglas
Training Spaniels · Joe Irving
Woodland Management for Pheasants and Wildlife · Nigel Gray